THE MEDICINAL CHEF
PLANT-BASED DIET

THE MEDICINAL CHEF

PLANT-BASED DIET

How to eat vegan & stay healthy

DALE PINNOCK

hamlyn

This book is dedicated to: Tanya Murkett, Ramsay and Candy, Nick Salt, Dr Alan Desmond, Dr Gemma Newman, all of my students on the 'Diploma in Culinary Medicine' course, and all of the readers that have supported my work over the years.

First published in Great Britain in 2021 by Hamlyn,
a division of Octopus Publishing Group Ltd,
Carmelite House, 50 Victoria Embankment,
London EC4Y 0DZ
www.octopusbooks.co.uk
www.octopusbooksusa.com

An Hachette UK Company
www.hachette.co.uk

Distributed in the US by Hachette Book Group, 1290 Avenue of the Americas, 4th and 5th Floors, New York, NY 10104

Distributed in Canada by Canadian Manda Group, 664 Annette St., Toronto, Ontario, Canada M6S 2C8

978-0-600-63604-5

A CIP catalogue record for this book is available from the British Library.

Printed and bound in China.

10 9 8 7 6 5 4 3 2 1

Editorial Director: Eleanor Maxfield
Senior Editor: Leanne Bryan
Deputy Art Director: Jaz Bahra
Copy Editor: Sophie Elletson
Design & Art Direction: Smith & Gilmour
Photographer: Faith Mason
Food Stylist: Phil Mundy
Props Stylist: Smith & Gilmour
Production Manager: Caroline Alberti

CONTENTS

INTRODUCTION

Let's start with a very important statement. I want to be real with you. I am not a vegan. I am not 100 per cent plant based. I am omnivorous, although plants do make up more than 80 per cent of my diet. I have written this book for two reasons. First and foremost, I have had thousands of requests for guidance on how to adopt a plant-based diet effectively, healthily and safely. Secondly, I have seen many people in the weird world of social media spread half-truths and make fundamental mistakes, and so I wanted to add to the body of work and help as many people as I can to embrace a plant-based diet in a way that will give them all of the benefits, while avoiding the common pitfalls. As a final note, this book is written only from a nutrition and health perspective. There is no comment, exploration or stance when it comes to ethics or moral positioning. That is not my argument.

The number of people moving towards a plant-based diet, or more specifically towards a vegan diet, quadrupled between 2014 and 2019 in the UK. In 2020, almost 2 per cent of the population – that's around a million people – identified as vegan. This shift has been driven by many motives, but one of the front runners is the impact on our health. When done right, a plant-based diet can indeed offer some considerable health benefits.

When we look at the food we eat, there are clear nutritional heroes as well as villains. It is pretty much a given that living on takeaways and fast food, day in, day out is going to lead us down a dangerous path. Processed foods contain an abundance of harmful substances (such as saturated fats, trans fats and sodium), and are pretty much devoid of micronutrients and the good stuff. So, the importance of adopting a wholefood diet is obvious. Out of everything that we find in a good wholefood diet, plants are among the true nutritional heroes. Now, as I said, I am omnivorous, so I appreciate the nutritional value of other foods, but I really do stand by the fact that plants are the superheroes of any diet. We all know they deliver vast amounts of vitamins, minerals and other important substances – but so do other foods. For example, plants offer antioxidants, but so does seafood. What sets plants apart is that they are packed to the rafters, to bursting point, with an extremely beneficial group of compounds. Enter phytochemicals.

Phytochemicals are substances that are unique to plants. They aren't strictly nutrients, as we have no set need for them and cannot be deficient in them, but they do influence our physiology – sometimes profoundly so. They can deliver almost drug-like effects in the body, and indeed many of the most common and well-known herbal medicines are so powerful because of their phytochemical profile. This is why plants have that extra edge: their propensity to protect our health. Turn to page 62 for a concise glossary of common phytochemicals, what they do and which foods you'll find them in.

A HEALTHY, WHOLEFOOD, PLANT-BASED DIET

Before we take a look at some of the documented ways in which a plant-based diet can benefit our health, it is important that we clarify what a healthy, wholefood, plant-based diet actually looks like. I don't want to be patronizing or seem as if I'm stating the obvious, but many people adopt a vegan diet with the assumption that the absence of animal products will in itself give rise to the associated health benefits. There is an element of truth in that, but only to a degree. In some situations, avoiding animal foods will lead to a mild improvement in some health markers, but a diet that is focused on refined foods as a substitute for these animal foods, such as white rice and pasta or sugary snacks, is no healthier than a diet that contains lots of meat. Just because it's vegan, doesn't mean it's healthy! The real crux here, regardless of whether you do choose to eat a little meat or fish now and then, is wholefoods, especially whole plants. So, let's look at the fundamental foods that should, for most of us at least, be present in our diet every day to enable us to really get the best out of this super-healthy way of eating.

WHOLEGRAINS

Grains can be such a minefield because of their carbohydrate content. There is a lot of debate surrounding carbohydrates, and even after almost 20 years of thriving on a mostly plant-based diet, I began to buy into the idea that carbohydrates were unnecessary. But I soon realized that it is the *type* of carbohydrate, as well as the amount we eat and what they are combined with, that makes the difference – and this has been a fundamental element of my work ever since.

So, let's unpack this a little bit. The carbohydrates that present real issues to our bodies are the refined variety. These are the ones that have had their fibre removed – think white rice, white bread, white pasta, and so on. These grains, or the grains used to make these products, have had their husks removed. The end result is a carbohydrate source from which it really doesn't take a great deal of digestive effort to liberate the simple sugars that make up these starchy foods. When we eat them, they flood our bodies with glucose (sugar). When our blood sugar rises, the pancreas secretes the hormone insulin. This will bind to an insulin receptor, which then opens a doorway in our cells called a glucose transporter. This allows cells to take up glucose to use as energy, which in turn brings our blood sugar down into normal ranges again. So far, so good. However, a problem arises if these foods make up the bulk of the diet: for example, a bowl of corn-based cereal and a slice of white toast for breakfast, a sandwich for lunch and a big bowl of white pasta for dinner. Now, this isn't unusual – in fact, it's very common – but when we consistently eat refined grains, and our blood sugar is consistently being pushed too high, things can start to break down over time.

Firstly, cells can only take in so much glucose in one sitting. This means the normal insulin response described above will only go on for so long. Once the cells are full, if blood-sugar levels are still too high, this still needs to be dealt with. So, it's sent to the liver to get turned into an easy-to-access stored form of energy: treacly glycerol, aka triglycerides. These are stored

in our fat tissue for later use – although seldom do we go for long enough periods without eating or in sufficient caloric deficit that this stored energy is accessed. This means too many refined carbs can cause weight gain. But the even deadlier part of this picture is that triglycerides are transported to the adipose (fat) tissue via the circulatory system. Raised triglycerides will increase LDL ('bad') cholesterol and are also susceptible to oxidation, which can damage blood vessel walls and set the scene for cardiovascular disease.

Okay, I know that was a lot of information, but the simple take-home is that too many refined carbohydrates will send blood-sugar levels up too high for too long, which can lead to weight gain and an increased risk of cardiovascular disease.

Wholegrains are a different beast to refined grains. These should be the only option when choosing your daily carbohydrates. Always choose wholegrain versions of staples such as bread and pasta. These have their fibre intact and a very high fibre level to begin with, so they take a lot more digestive effort. This means they liberate their glucose far more slowly, which in turn means that the body is drip-fed with glucose rather than flooded – they are low-glycaemic carbohydrates. This gradual increase of blood sugar means that cells are more able to cope with the amount of incoming glucose: they don't get full in the same way. The wave of negative events I described above also doesn't happen. Well, it would if you ate too many wholegrains, but it is difficult to overeat them, because fibre is so filling. Providing your plate is balanced, it's unlikely you'll eat too many. Wholegrains should take up (at the very most) a quarter of your plate at each meal. This same caveat applies for other starchy foods, such as sweet potatoes, white potatoes, parsnips, yams and cassava.

The final point is that wholegrains are very rich in some key nutrients. The top of this list are the B vitamins. These are vital for our health and play many roles in the body. They are essential for turning food into energy, manufacturing neurotransmitters and influencing mood, to name but a few benefits. Wholegrains are generally high in a few key minerals too, such as zinc (see page 23), magnesium (see page 52) and iron (see page 24).

BEANS AND PULSES

It is going to come as no surprise that beans and pulses are staples in this big picture. There is a good reason that they are the base of so many plant-based dishes.

Beans and pulses are a super-versatile source of protein. Having a good source of protein at each meal will, of course, provide essential amino acids, but, keeping the issue of balanced blood sugar in mind, a good-quality protein combined with a good-quality low-glycaemic carbohydrate will further slow down digestion. This is because protein decreases the rate at which blood sugar rises.

Beans and pulses are also a great source of B vitamins, iron, magnesium and zinc.

Where pulses definitely come into their own is their fibre content: they are full of it. This has several benefits. A superficial benefit is that it helps to keep us feeling fuller for longer, which is all good, but there is far more to it than that. The fibre content of beans and pulses (and, in all fairness, all plant foods) can bind to cholesterol in the digestive tract and carry it out of the body via the bowel. This is explained in more detail later in the book (see page 45), but long story short, it will result in the lowering of cholesterol levels.

The other big area where fibre comes into play is in supporting the health of the gut flora. Fibre works as a food source for gut bacteria and helps them to flourish. When our gut bacteria feed on fibre, they release by-products that are essential for the health of the gut. This too is explained in more detail later in the book.

Like starches, beans and pulses should make up no more than a quarter of your plate.

LEAFY GREENS AND NON-STARCHY VEGETABLES

These are what will make up the bulk of your plate. They are the powerhouses of a plant-based diet, as they are where you will find the micronutrients. Carbohydrates and proteins are the key macronutrients, our energy and repair/maintenance nutrients. But micronutrients – vitamins, minerals, trace elements – are the sparks of life. Micronutrients are biochemical facilitators. This means that, in the body, they either directly make something happen – i.e. a specific chemical reaction or event – or they make something that makes something happen – i.e. they help convert amino acids to neurotransmitters, which then carry chemical messages around the body via the nerve cells. An adequate intake of all micronutrients is essential for optimal health, as each nutrient has a specific role in your body. They have a role in all body processes, from energy production to immune function, and from bone health to fluid balance.

When looking at your plate, half of what is on there should be leafy greens. Think:
- Kale
- Cavolo nero
- Spinach
- Cabbage
- Broccoli

When it comes to the other non-starchy vegetables, think anything that grows above ground:
- Peppers
- Tomatoes
- Courgettes
- Aubergines
- Mushrooms

POTENTIAL PITFALLS AND COMMON MYTHS

Before we dive deep into the many ways in which a plant-based diet can benefit our health, we must be completely frank about the potential pitfalls that are associated with this way of eating. There aren't many, and luckily they can all be addressed once we know how. There are a few nutrients that are hard to get on a plant-based diet and will require supplementation, and there's one myth to bust.

VITAMIN B12

Let's start with the most obvious and well-known nutrient that cannot be obtained from a plant-based diet – no matter what someone trying to sell you a weird and wonderful 'superfood' might claim. This water-soluble nutrient is found only in animal foods. Strangely, it is actually derived from bacteria found in soil, so most grazing animals get their B12 from non-animal sources, and then store it effectively in their tissues. The cleanliness protocols surrounding food production nowadays remove any trace of these bacteria from plant foods.

B12 is a nutrient that is vital for the production of red blood cells. A long-term lack of B12 can give rise to a state called megaloblastic anaemia. This is where the bone marrow begins to produce large, abnormal, immature red blood cells with reduced oxygen-carrying capacity. Red blood cells contain the protein haemoglobin. Oxygen binds to this protein and is then transported to our cells and tissues to support their metabolic needs. This is one of the reasons B12 deficiency can lead to fatigue. The red blood cells are less capable of delivering oxygen, which in turns affects the amount of energy that tissues can produce over time.

B12 is also involved in protecting the health of the brain, the heart and the cardiovascular system.

It is important to note that many people believe they are fine and that their B12 levels are not an issue if they aren't feeling any of the effects associated with low levels. This is because out of all of the B vitamins, B12 is the only one that can be stored in the body. There is a B12 pool in the liver which can last as long as six years in some cases, so it can take some time for signs of deficiency to show.

There is only one way to ensure you get enough, without question or argument. Supplement! 100–200mcg daily will keep your B12 at a healthy level.

LONG-CHAIN OMEGA-3 FATTY ACIDS

These vital fat-derived substances are essential for the health of every system in the body. They are the key building blocks for a group of communication compounds called prostaglandins, which help to regulate inflammation, pain signalling and smooth muscle contraction. They also produce another group of anti-inflammatory substances called resolvins. Omega-3 fatty acids, specifically a type called DHA, can also play a structural role in the body. DHA is an integral part of key structures in the eyes, the membranes of our cells and the myelin sheath of the central nervous system.

When it comes to a plant-based diet, we need to address long-chain omega-3 fatty acids. While omega 3 certainly can be found in a plant-based diet, we need to accept a very inconvenient truth: omega 3 is not just one substance, it is a whole family of substances. In our bodies, we need DHA and EPA, another long-chain omega 3, to feed into the metabolic pathways that give rise to the all-important prostaglandins and resolvins. In plants, omega 3 exists in the form of ALA, which is more of a medium-chain omega-3 fatty acid. ALA needs to go through significant enzymatic conversion to form EPA and DHA. The problem is, the human body is incredibly poor at doing this conversion. On average, the conversion rate of ALA into EPA is around 4–6 per cent, while ALA into DHA is around 0.4 per cent. The conversion may be higher in women compared to men and higher still in pregnant women. But what this means is that you could eat plant sources of omega 3 (such as flaxseeds and chia seeds) all day long, but the poor conversion of their ALA into the long-chain varieties that our bodies can actually use would leave you with only the tiniest of traces. It would be nowhere near enough to give you what you need for good health. I don't care how many times someone tries to tell you that flaxseeds and chia seeds are a great source of omega 3 – it's simply not true, because our ability to put it to use just isn't there. They are wonderful foods for a whole host of other reasons – they're high in fibre, minerals and potent phytochemicals – but they are not a good source of omega 3.

PLANT-BASED OMEGA 3

For a long time, the only way to actually get those vital long-chain omega-3 fatty acids into your system was to eat oily fish and grass-fed cattle, as they eat the plant-derived ALA and convert it very efficiently into the long-chain EPA and DHA. These are stored in their tissues, which we then eat. However, this is clearly not an option for someone who wants to follow a 100 per cent plant-based diet. Thankfully, there is now a new option: supplements made from algae that contain both EPA and DHA. There are many on the market now, although it's only recently that a vegan EPA has been produced (DHA has been easier to formulate). I really do strongly advise you to seek out one of these supplements. Look for one that contains around 700mg of omega 3 from algae.

There are other nutrients that are not necessarily an issue for everyone following a plant-based diet, but are still on the potential watch list.

ZINC

Zinc is a hugely important mineral. It's found in every cell in the body and is a significant component of over 200 different enzymes.

One area where zinc really does shine is immunity. While supplements such as vitamin C have had mixed results in trials as a remedy for the common cold, zinc has fared better. Zinc is used by our white blood cells, the foot soldiers of the immune system, to code genes that essentially control the way in which these cells respond to pathogens, and the types of responses they deliver. Zinc also has antiviral properties in its own right.

This wonder nutrient is vital for proper cell division, and as such plays an essential role in pregnancy, in fetal development. Low zinc levels in the mother have been linked to premature birth, low birth weight and poor growth rates.

Zinc is also vital for almost every aspect of male sexual function. A lack of zinc can lead to lower testosterone levels, because zinc is vital for its manufacture and metabolism. Zinc is also necessary for healthy sperm count and motility.

It's also an essential nutrient for skin health and it can benefit the skin in two main ways. Firstly, it has a regulatory role in sebaceous secretions – the production of oil in the skin. If the skin is too oily, then adequate zinc intake can reduce sebum production. Conversely, if the skin is too dry, adequate zinc intake can *increase* sebum secretion to balance the skin out. The other way that zinc can benefit the skin is in relation to acne. Zinc has the power to fight infection, and acne is an infection of the pilosebaceous unit (this is the name for the area where the hair follicle and sebaceous gland meet, and is the area that becomes inflamed when a spot forms). Therefore, supporting the immune system by maintaining good levels of zinc can clear this infection faster.

There isn't a vast array of plant-based sources that contain substantial levels of zinc. The foods that are most abundant are nuts and seeds, such as walnuts, Brazil nuts, pumpkin seeds and sunflower seeds. If you eat these regularly, you shouldn't have any issues with zinc levels. However, many people following a low-calorie plant-based diet avoid these foods because of their high oil content. But I really do not recommend this, because they contain such a vast array of nutrients, so do eat these nuts and seeds. Other plant-based sources of zinc include quinoa, chickpeas and lentils. If you choose to supplement with zinc, it's 15mg for women and 30mg for men daily (men need extra for normal testosterone metabolism).

IRON

Iron is essential for human health, and deficiency can have serious consequences. There absolutely is iron in plant foods; it's known as non-haem iron.

The primary function of iron in the body is to transport oxygen to our tissues. On the surface of our red blood cells, we have four proteins bound together to form a structure called haemoglobin. On each of these proteins within haemoglobin, there are sites where iron attaches. In turn, the iron binds to oxygen when it enters the body from the lungs, and the red blood cells carry it to the cells and tissues that need it.

Iron deficiency leads to the condition known as anaemia. This can manifest as fatigue, muscle weakness and general lack of energy. Sufferers can also experience shortness of breath and heart palpitations, and often present with pale skin. Deficiency in iron can be a particular concern in women who have a heavy flow during their period, as the blood loss (and therefore iron loss) at this time is notable. In fact, many women in this situation do sit on the border of anaemia. An iron-rich diet or a supplement is often advised in such circumstances. If you decide to supplement, look for a product with around 15mg iron bisglycinate.

There is some debate around non-haem iron versus the haem iron in animal foods. Non-haem iron is thought to be less bioavailable – i.e. absorbed less efficiently – than haem iron, and therefore we need more of it.

When it comes to non-haem iron, you need to maximize your intake and maximize your absorption. Make dark leafy greens a focal part of your diet, as these are generally the richest sources of non-haem iron. Whenever you consume these, ensure you have a good source of vitamin C alongside, because vitamin C helps us to absorb more of the iron present. This could be as simple as a squeeze of lemon juice over a spinach salad. Other iron-rich plant-based foods include lentils, chickpeas, beans, tofu and tempeh, pumpkin and sesame seeds, oats and quinoa.

THE PROTEIN MYTH

The last thing to discuss is probably the greatest myth surrounding a plant-based diet: that we can't get enough protein if we don't eat meat. (I also discuss the myth around calcium in the Skeletal Health section on page 50.) The number one question when it comes to plant-based diets is probably: 'But where do you get your protein?' There is a commonly held belief that if we are not eating slabs of meat or cheese, then we suddenly become protein deficient.

Of course, true protein deficiency is real and can manifest as a condition called kwashiorkor, but this is something that we usually only see occurring in developing countries. This level of protein malnutrition is serious and arises only when there is immense food scarcity and lack of food variety, which is unlikely to ever happen to anyone in the developed world. Eating a plant-based diet does not result in protein deficiency. Let me explain why.

Proteins are built from amino acids, just like houses are made from bricks assembled together to build inner and outer walls and arches. There are 20 different amino acids that are used to manufacture human proteins. Of these, nine must come from our diet, and the rest our body can make. Proteins can be relatively simple, such as enzymes, or they can be larger and denser, such as skeletal muscle. Regardless, they are all sequences of amino acids stuck together in varying degrees of size and complexity. Now, for some reason, there is a belief that when we gobble down a steak, it will get digested and turned into human protein. But nope – not quite! Instead, these complex proteins will be digested and some of their constituent amino acids will be liberated. These amino acids then head to the liver and join the amino acid pool, which acts like a warehouse. As and when we need to manufacture a particular protein, the liver will access this pool and string together specific amino acids in the specific sequence and amount necessary to make the protein in question. So, meat is digested, which liberates its constituent amino acids, which get sent to storage and reassembled to make human proteins.

Remember when I said that nine of these amino acids need to come from the diet? These are known as 'essential' amino acids. Animal proteins contain all of these essential amino acids, and are considered to be 'complete' proteins. Plant proteins, on the other hand, do not tend to contain all the essential amino acids (with some exceptions, including soy, quinoa and buckwheat), and are therefore considered to be 'incomplete' proteins. This is one of the reasons that some people believe plant-based foods to be an inferior source of protein.

However, if you're eating a balanced wholefood, plant-based diet, you will get all nine of the essential amino acids, and then your body can manufacture the remaining eleven. Obviously, if you live on chips and biscuits, while you technically might be eating a plant-based diet, you aren't exactly flooding your body with nutrient-dense foods, so the key here is that your diet needs to be balanced. As long as you are eating fruits, vegetables, wholegrains, beans and pulses, and nuts and seeds daily, you really have little to worry about.

A NOTE

To maintain long-term metabolic health, it is essential to have a protein source with each meal. Your plate should have a slow-release (low-glycaemic) carbohydrate source, a good-quality protein source (such as beans, tofu, tempeh, etc.) and an abundance of non-starchy vegetables. This creates a meal that will take a long time to digest, which will not only keep you feeling fuller for longer, but will also control your blood sugar. If you ate, say, just a plate of potatoes and rice (although there is nothing wrong with either of those foods individually), that plate of pure starch really won't require much digestive effort to liberate its glucose content. This means your blood sugar will shoot through the roof and cause havoc. Now, once in a while, this is of little consequence, as the worst problem it will cause is a bit of light-headedness, an energy slump and general grogginess when your blood-sugar levels eventually crash back down. However, if this dietary pattern is followed day after day, year in, year out, it can have a serious metabolic impact. A high-glycaemic diet can raise triglycerides and LDL cholesterol, increase blood pressure and eventually reduce the effectiveness of the insulin system, setting the stage for type 2 diabetes. You can prevent all of this by simply ensuring you get some good-quality protein, some slow-release carbohydrates and lots of non-starchy veg at each meal.

TO CONCLUDE

Now that we have looked at what the basics are and addressed the potential pitfalls of a plant-based diet, let's explore the exciting stuff – the ways in which a wholefood, plant-based diet can actually benefit our health! Now, one caveat here. There are literally thousands of anecdotal reports of how adopting a plant-based diet has led to vast improvements in a massive array of health conditions. I don't doubt these, but what I have included here are the key ways that such a diet can assist our health from the point of view of available research and established data. So, if you are thinking 'but why haven't you mentioned X or Y?', it is because the data is anecdotal or scant.

Let's start with the obvious.

THE
SCIENCE

DIGESTIVE HEALTH

The digestive system can be rapidly influenced by diet and lifestyle. It is incredibly responsive to what we eat, and a poor diet can result in anything from minor annoyances to severe illnesses of the gut. A plant-based diet has been well documented as being beneficial to multiple aspects of digestive health.

FIBRE

When it comes to the health of the digestive system, the most important nutrient that a plant-centric diet delivers is fibre. The first and most obvious way in which fibre benefits digestive health is the simple matter of improved intestinal transit. Around one in seven UK adults suffer from constipation. In the short term, this can be rather uncomfortable, causing bloating and discomfort, but in the long term, it can raise the risk of all manner of problems, from haemorrhoids caused by pressure build-up to bowel cancer.

Dietary fibre is great at absorbing many times its own weight in water. This causes it to increase in volume and stretch the walls of the gut. When this occurs, stretch receptors in the gut wall are stimulated. This triggers peristalsis, which is the orchestrated rhythmical sequence of contractions that move the intestinal contents along to the finish line. Fibre helps to both soften the stool and ensure that gut transit time is in a healthy range.

THE ROLE OF OUR GUT FLORA

The most exciting thing about dietary fibre (yes... there really is something exciting about it!) is the impact that it has on our gut flora. Before we go into depth about this, let's familiarize ourselves with the gut flora and the many roles that it can play.

The digestive system is not simply an empty tube: it is a whole ecosystem containing in the region of 100 trillion bacterial cells.

Some are what could be thought of as bad or problematic, but the highest proportion of them are what we would consider beneficial. These have a symbiotic relationship with us – meaning that we benefit from them, and they benefit from us. There can be anywhere between 300 and 1,000 different species of bacteria living in the gut.

Immunity

The 'good bacteria', as they have become known, have a defensive role to play. For a long time, they have been known to be a vital part of immunity within the gut, as they are one of the first barriers faced by pathogens entering the body via the digestive tract. They offer an immediate and localized defence. However, in recent years we have realized that the effect of gut flora on immunity goes far beyond just a local influence. We now know that the bacterial colony of the gut can influence immunity systemically. The bacteria in your gut can literally influence a white blood cell in your little toe. See the section on Immune Health on page 46 for a deeper look at this.

Appetite

It also appears that your gut bacterial colony can have a significant influence on your appetite. This is because they can influence the production of several appetite-suppressing hormones, such as peptide YY (PYY), GLP-1 and leptin.[1] These hormones are released when we have eaten an adequate amount of food in one sitting. Some cases of obesity have been linked to low levels, or at least dysfunctional production, of these hormones.

Nutrient synthesis

Our gut flora can actually synthesize certain nutrients too – the main ones being B vitamins. There is some debate, however, as to whether we can actually absorb the nutrients that are synthesized in the gut – but nature seldom does things for the sake of it, so it is likely that we can utilize them.

HOW FIBRE BENEFITS OUR GUT FLORA

While most of us are aware that fibre 'keeps things moving', few of us realize that fibre is actually the cornerstone for a healthy and flourishing bacterial colony within the digestive tract. This is because fibre is composed of an array of different carbohydrates. Some are so dense that they simply pass through us intact (insoluble fibre). Then there are other types of fibre that are a little too complex to simply be broken down by pancreatic enzymes for absorption in the small intestine; instead, they get broken down in the bowel, by our gut bacteria. This is done by means of saccharolytic fermentation, where the gut bacteria begin to feed on these types of complex-carbohydrate chains. This helps to break them down, but also helps our gut bacteria to grow and flourish by providing a food source for them. These types of carbohydrates are called prebiotics and include inulin, oligosaccharides and soluble fibre.

This is where a particular variety of dietary fibre really does have some very profound effects. Remember I said that this was a symbiotic relationship? Well, we certainly benefit from this process too. When gut bacteria ferment these carbohydrates, a group of by-products are released called short-chain fatty acids. Short-chain fatty acids, such as butyrate and propionate, have an impressive array of positive health benefits.

Butyrate

Unlike most other cells in our body, which use glucose as a fuel source, the cells in our colon mainly use butyrate. Butyrate helps to ensure these cells are functioning optimally and, importantly, that they can maintain themselves in a healthy manner. Butyrate also reduces the local oxygen levels, which helps our good bacteria to thrive. Elevated butyrate also increases the production of glutathione, a potent antioxidant. These are thought to be some of the major reasons why higher-fibre diets are associated with reduced bowel cancer risk.

In addition, butyrate helps to strengthen the tight junctions in the gut, a series of protein bands that secure the space between enterocytes (the cells that make up the gut wall). These cells

have to be tightly packed together so that the gut can control what passes through, with absorption sites and processes for nutrients. If partially digested food items and pathogens were able to squeeze between the gaps in these cells and enter the blood (pathogens frequently do that in other tissues), they would cause severe immunological challenges. To prevent this from happening, tight junctions like bungee ropes pull these cells together. These tight junctions can be damaged by poor diet and inflammation. When this occurs, a condition crudely named 'leaky gut' can arise. This isn't, of course, an actual leaky gut, but more a gut environment that has less protection against foreign materials entering the systemic circulation and causing an issue.

Propionate

This short-chain fatty acid is known to have a notable influence on appetite. It causes a rise in the production of the hormones PYY and GLP-1 from colonocytes (cells lining the colon).[2] These are the satiety hormones that tell us when we have eaten enough and prevent overeating.

POLYPHENOLS

One of the major things that makes plant-centric diets so healthy is the vast array of phytochemicals that are present. They are the major bonuses of plant foods, as they can have profound beneficial effects on our physiology.

Among the most abundant phytochemical groups are polyphenols. These are colour pigments in foods, and you will see them again and again in this book. Polyphenols also have a role to play in supporting gut health, and this is all down to – surprise, surprise – their interactions with our gut flora.

Polyphenols appear to have a prebiotic effect, promoting the growth and flourishing of good bacteria, and also seem to create an environment less favourable for more harmful bacterial strains.

Our gut flora transforms polyphenols into bioactive substances that can deliver this selective beneficial activity.[3]

The simple addition to your diet of plenty of brightly coloured fruit and veg can flood your system with polyphenols – and therefore promote good gut health. Flavonoids, isoflavonoids and lignans are all part of the polyphenol family.

WHEN A PLANT-BASED DIET MAY NOT BE SUITABLE

There is one very small group of people who may find that a typical plant-based diet is not suitable for them. These are people who have issues with FODMAPs. FODMAP stands for: fermentable oligosaccharides, disaccharides, monosaccharides and polyols. These are the types of carbohydrate that are the main players in everything we have discussed – the varieties that require bacterial fermentation to break them down. In individuals who are sensitive to FODMAPs, this fermentation can cause bloating and pain, and can also rapidly draw water into the colon, causing aggressive diarrhoea.

While it is possible to adhere to a plant-based diet while avoiding FODMAPs, anyone with FODMAP issues should be under the guidance of a specialist dietitian.

CARDIOVASCULAR HEALTH

Heart disease is the biggest killer in the Western world. Period. While there are shocking stats that one in two of us will be affected by cancer (I know!), it is still cardiovascular disease that claims more lives. Because cancer-screening techniques have improved, it can be detected earlier and more people are surviving because we can do something about it. The same can, of course, be said for cardiovascular disease, but often the first sign that anything is wrong is, in fact, a fatal heart attack. It is a disease that silently simmers beneath the surface, and unless we are monitoring markers like inflammatory mediators, triglycerides and total blood lipids, we are unable to know when things are starting to go wrong. A simple cholesterol test once a year that just gives you a single number doesn't tell you much at all, so most people are unaware that disease is developing.

Right, that's the doom and gloom out of the way, but I had to set the scene to bring all of this into context. The beauty of a wholefood, plant-based diet is that it can drastically influence many of the risk factors for cardiovascular disease and directly intervene in – and prevent – many of the physiological events that can lead to it. This means that a wholefood, plant-based diet is probably the number one most effective intervention for the prevention of cardiovascular disease. The American physician and researcher Dr Dean Ornish has, over the last few decades, published vast amounts of research, including peer-reviewed clinical research, showing that, with a carefully constructed wholefood, plant-based diet, cardiovascular disease can be not only prevented and managed, but clinically reversed. There are several factors at play here, which we'll explore in the coming pages.

THE POWER OF POLYPHENOLS

As I have explained, polyphenols are among the most abundant groups of phytochemicals found in a wholefood, plant-based diet. These are what give fruits and vegetables their bright colours, and they can range from off-whites and greens through to the deep ruby reds, purples and near-black hues that we find in many berries and soft fruits. All members of the polyphenol family have benefits for the cardiovascular system, but it's a particular group called the flavonoids, the ones that deliver the reds and dark purples, that are the true heroes when it comes to keeping the cardiovascular system healthy. This is all thanks to the influence they have upon the endothelium, the bioactive inner skin that lines the blood vessels.

Flavonoids interact directly with the endothelium. At the University of Reading in the UK, Professor Jeremy Spencer is a leading researcher in the field of flavonoids and cardiovascular health. The research has shown that flavonoids are quite readily absorbed by the endothelial cells. When endothelial cells take up flavonoids, the flavonoids cause quite a degree of metabolic distress within the cell. This, in turn, causes the endothelial cells to secrete more nitric oxide, which is important for regulating blood pressure. Remember, the endothelium isn't just a simple barrier; it is highly active tissue. Nitric oxide leaves the endothelial cells and then migrates into the wall of the blood vessel, which is composed of layered smooth muscle fibres. As the nitric oxide migrates into the smooth muscle, it causes those fibres to relax. As the fibres relax, the blood vessel widens. As the blood vessel widens, and because the amount of blood in that vessel hasn't changed, the pressure against the vessel wall decreases. In short, nitric oxide lowers blood pressure. This is a transient effect, and clearly will not take the place of a drug any time soon, but it does demonstrate how, armed with the right information, we can take steps towards looking after our own health with our lifestyle choices. Many of Reading University's trials have been published.[4]

The benefits of nitric oxide go a step further. The first stage of cardiovascular disease is endothelial damage. Nitric oxide helps to protect the endothelium, making it a little more resilient to inflammatory damage. It is this localized inflammatory damage that is the first stage of vascular injury, and eventually gives rise to lesions and plaques within blood vessels. If this is prevented or minimized, then so is risk. An increase in plant intake, especially within the framework of a Mediterranean-style diet, consistently shows an increase in nitric oxide expression.[5]

POTASSIUM BOOST

A good-quality wholefood, plant-based diet is a very rich source of the mineral potassium. This is a vital mineral for so many aspects of human physiology, but is of special importance to the cardiovascular system. For starters, it controls every single beat of your heart. Every last one. It fires the nerve fibres that envelop the heart, triggering the muscle to contract. It also plays a very important role in regulating blood pressure. For hypertensive (high blood pressure) individuals, moving over to a diet rich in potassium can lower systolic blood pressure more than 10 points. This is partially due to the influence that it has on smooth muscle function, but a great deal of this effect comes from the dance between sodium and potassium in the kidneys.

In the kidney there is a filtration system called the nephron. It filters the blood to remove waste products that are then excreted via the urine. Potassium and sodium influence the speed at which fluid moves through the kidneys. Sodium slows down the movement of fluid through the nephron, whereas potassium speeds it up. When our diets are high in sodium but low in potassium, as is the case with the typical Western diet, or certainly a diet that is heavily centred around processed and convenience foods, then we are in a state where the movement of fluid through the nephron slows considerably. This not only puts a strain on the kidneys over time, but can also cause us

to retain fluid. This is why many people report a puffy face or abdomen or swollen fingers after eating a lot of salty food. The problem here is that by retaining fluid, the watery portion of our blood, the plasma, increases in volume. This means that the volume of blood in the blood vessels increases and blood pressure goes up. Sodium adds further insult to injury, though, because it is vasoconstrictive, which means it causes contraction of the blood vessels. Normally, vessels have a certain amount of 'give' in them, and the increase in blood volume will simply cause them to stretch a little, meaning the pressure increase against the vessel wall is less problematic. However, if the blood vessel is strongly contracted from vasoconstriction, then an increase in blood volume has the potential to be cataclysmic.

Potassium, on the other hand, speeds up the movement of fluid through the nephrons in the kidneys. It can ease fluid retention. In fact, many of the more simple diuretic drugs contain potassium, and the traditional use of dandelion leaf as a diuretic is down it being so rich in potassium. When our intake of potassium is higher than or matched with our intake of sodium, we don't put undue strain on the kidneys, and so don't run the risk of holding on to excess fluid and our blood pressure increasing.

Potassium also has the benefit of being vasodilatory, meaning it causes blood vessels to dilate – just like the flavonoids – which helps to reduce pressure against the vessel walls.

Bananas and green veg are especially high in potassium.

FANTASTIC FIBRE

One of the broadest benefits of a plant-based diet is the high levels of fibre that it provides. Fibre is so often overlooked when it comes to cardiovascular health. We automatically (and rightfully, of course) see it as something that is mostly relevant to digestive health and weight management. However, it is also a real player in long-term cardiovascular health.

Fibre is one of the best things that we can consume to safeguard long-term cardiovascular health, and thankfully it is something that is abundant in a wholefood, plant-based diet. There are two types of fibre: soluble and insoluble. The insoluble variety is what used to be called 'roughage' (awful word), and it is the variety that comes out the other end fully intact.

SOLUBLE FIBRE

Soluble fibre actually breaks down and takes on many times its own weight in water. When this happens, it forms a gel-like substance in the gut, which can bind to cholesterol and carry it away via the bowel. Now, this isn't cholesterol from food. When we hear about X or Y being a high-cholesterol food, we needn't worry. It was proved in the '80s that food sources of cholesterol have zero impact upon serum levels of cholesterol. What we are talking about here is cholesterol that the body has already made.

Cholesterol is made in the liver. It is a vital substance in the body. All of our steroidal hormones (for example, testosterone and oestrogen) are made from it. It is also part of the structure of cell membranes. We need it, but we also need to ensure that its production and distribution does not go haywire, especially when coupled with other negative metabolic states, such as systemic inflammation. A small amount of the cholesterol made will leave the liver and go directly into circulation. The rest will be used to create bile salts that are used for the emulsification and breakdown of fats. Once the bile salts have fulfilled this role, they are then reabsorbed via the intestine, and the cholesterol is repurposed and put to other uses.

When soluble fibre binds to cholesterol/bile salts in the intestine, it creates a permanent bond. This prevents the repurposing of cholesterol, because the bile salts are carried away via the bowel instead. When this happens, the liver will place less cholesterol directly into circulation, with the end result being a lowering of serum cholesterol levels, which is why soluble fibre is particularly valuable when it comes to cardiovascular health. It is important to note, though, that there has to be a continual intake of fibre. The effects only last for as long as it is around.

IMMUNE HEALTH

Our immune system is made up of a complex array of different cells and tissues that defend us from pathogens, bugs and damaged cells. This system has multiple layers and can be influenced in many different ways by the foods that we eat. Plant-based diets can be beneficial to immune health; however, zinc, which is a hugely important mineral for the immune system, can be insufficient on a plant-based diet, and therefore we need to address this with the right effort and focus.

SUPPORTING THE GUT MICROBIOME

In my opinion, the number one way in which a plant-based or plant-dense diet can influence the health and functioning of our immune system is via the gut microbiome. As I outlined in the Digestive Health section, the array of complex fibre that a plant-based diet delivers will create an environment in which gut flora can flourish. Gut bacteria ferment and feed on the complex sugars that make these types of fibres, and, in doing so, they increase in number and diversity, as well as producing by-products that increase the health of the gut tissue.

So, why is this important to immunity? Firstly, our gut bacteria create a physical barrier between the contents of the digestive tract and the inner workings of the body. When you think about it, the digestive system is a very convenient route for potential pathogens to enter the body. By creating a protective film or 'biofilm' in the gut, our microbiome helps to stop these pathogens from getting anywhere by simply competing for space with them. This biofilm also covers so many potential routes of entry that many pathogens cannot get through.

The second stage of protection that our gut flora offer is the release of chemicals called bacteriocins. Even though our gut flora are bacteria themselves, they can secrete these chemicals, which can differentiate between beneficial bacteria and potentially pathogenic bacteria, and offer up a targeted chemical attack on bacteria that can cause illness.

Finally, we have an interplay between the gut microbiome and the development and maturation of juvenile immune cells (B and T cells). Differing strains of gut bacteria play an important role in these types of cells developing fully. This helps ensure beneficial levels of these immune cells are ready and waiting in circulation, meaning a healthy and well-functioning immune system.

DIETARY IMMUNOMODULATORS

Dietary fibre and gut interactions can go a step further in terms of immunity. There are specific types of polysaccharides (large, complex sugar molecules) called beta-glucans that can influence a huge array of immune responses; in fact, beta-glucans are considered a potential drug[6] based on the extent of clinical research.

Beta-glucans are found in some grains, such as oats, but in abundance in mushrooms, with shiitake and maitake varieties being the richest sources. They have a fascinating interaction with the lymphatics of the gut. Throughout the wall of the gut, there are little surveillance stations known as Peyer's patches. These are little patches of tissue that monitor gut contents and report their findings to the rest of the immune system. They contain cells such as dendritic cells, and Th0 cells, both of which can report different findings and systemically instigate specific and relevant immune responses.

Beta-glucans resemble polysaccharides that are displayed on the outer surface of certain pathogens. This sets off an alarm response within the cell population of the Peyer's patches and causes them to release a cascade of chemicals called cytokines, which then recruit specific immune responses. Beta-glucans are known to increase natural killer cell production, reduce aggressive inflammatory responses and reduce antibody responses. This has many exciting clinical applications – see the article referenced on page 47 for a brilliant overview of these.

ZINC

The mineral zinc is an absolute fundamental for the health of the immune system. This is because it is used by our leukocytes, the white-blood-cell army of our immune system, to manufacture genes. These genes are like the software that runs the hardware (the cell), and they regulate the way in which our white blood cells respond to infection, ensuring they deliver an accurate and effective response. As we've seen, some plant-based diets can be quite notably deficient in zinc. See pages 23–4 for advice on how to incorporate zinc into your diet.

SKELETAL HEALTH

The skeleton is made out of a gelatinous lattice structure that forms the shape of our bones. This lattice has minerals embedded in it that solidify to form bone. This is in constant flux, and bone remodelling takes place almost continually. Cells called osteoclasts break down bone by dissolving the mineral matrix and liberating the minerals, then other cells called osteoblasts build new bone by laying down and solidifying minerals. This is influenced by homeostatic controls, hormones and also nutrition. For example, when blood calcium levels drop, osteoclasts will demineralize the skeleton to liberate some calcium, which can then enter circulation. Likewise, when we consume calcium-rich foods and blood calcium levels rise, vitamin D transports excess calcium from circulation to the skeleton and stimulates osteoblasts to get building and lay down this fresh supply. So, we must get this aspect of our diet right.

There is a myth that plant-based diets are a problem for long-term skeletal health – namely, that it's not possible to get enough calcium on a plant-based diet, because the best source of calcium is dairy foods. Although it may be true that those following a plant-based diet should be careful when it comes to bone health, it might not be for the reasons you think. But before we get into telling the real story, let us look at the key nutrients for skeletal health.

CALCIUM

Calcium is the basic structural component of the skeleton. It is the primary mineral that is laid down within the skeletal matrix to harden the skeleton so it can offer support and withstand force. While it is the most abundant mineral in the skeleton, however, it may actually be the least important when it comes to skeletal health. Liken calcium to the bricks on a building site: while they are the key structural component, without a team of builders and tradesmen, they will just sit there. Calcium is as good as useless without all the other auxiliary nutrients needed to do something with it. Most of the pathological processes of osteoporosis and osteomalacia/rickets involve, at some stage, the availability of calcium, whether through lack of dietary intake, lack of absorption or lack of mobilization to where it is needed. But all of this is regulated by other auxiliary nutrients. A good intake of calcium is essential, especially during key times, such as infancy and senior years, but calcium isn't the be-all and end-all for skeletal health.

Plant foods that are high in calcium include leafy greens, tofu and sesame seeds.

VITAMIN D

Vitamin D is certainly one of the big nutritional darlings of recent times and a nutrient that has been the focus of a great deal of research. It isn't strictly a vitamin; it is more of a hormone, as it is synthesized in the body and then delivers its actions in sites away from its point of synthesis. The primary source of vitamin D for humans is the conversion of cholesterol into vitamin D upon exposing the skin to ultraviolet radiation – the sun!

When the sun hits our skin, our skin synthesizes cholecalciferol, which is metabolically inactive. It needs to go through several stages of enzymatic conversion before it can even be used. It is converted into calcidiol in the liver, and then the kidneys convert this into calcitriol – the biologically active form. The converted calcitriol increases the concentration of calcium in the blood. If blood calcium goes down, calcitriol responds by increasing absorption of dietary calcium and also reducing calcium loss via the kidneys. This in itself can encourage greater bone remineralization, as more available calcium is presented.

To maintain healthy blood levels of vitamin D, aim to get 10–30 minutes of midday sunlight, several times per week. People with darker skin may need a little more than this.

We can get some vitamin D from our food. Foods that contain vitamin D are mainly animal products, including full-fat dairy, fatty fish and egg yolks. However, some plant-based foods, such as mushrooms, as well as fortified plant-based milks and tofu, contain small amounts of vitamin D.

MAGNESIUM

Magnesium is one of the most overlooked minerals in the bone-health picture. It is one of the most commonly deficient nutrients in the Western world. One of the reasons for this is that it is most abundant in green leafy vegetables – and how many people chow down huge amounts of greens every day? Couple this with the fact that it is used in over 300 enzymatic reactions in the body, meaning it can quickly be used up, and the stage for deficiency is set. Sixty per cent of our entire magnesium stores are found in the skeleton. In terms of its role in bone health, much of it is linked to facilitating enzymatic reactions. One of the first areas this comes into play is the conversion of vitamin D into its active form. Also, there is an enzyme that is required for forming calcium crystals within the skeleton, called alkaline phosphatase. Magnesium is an important component for activating this enzyme, and even a mild deficiency can lead to abnormal crystal formation.

ZINC

In recent years it has come to light that the mineral zinc is a key player in the health of the skeleton. Zinc is an important cofactor in the stimulation of osteoblasts and can even stimulate the production of new osteoblasts. Zinc appears to aid in the

suppression of excessive osteoclast activity and can help trigger apoptosis (programmed cell death) in old osteoclasts. This promotes good bone health. Like magnesium, zinc is also involved in the activity of the enzyme alkaline phosphatase, which is required for forming calcium crystals within the skeleton.

See pages 23–4 for advice on how to incorporate zinc into your diet.

VITAMIN K

There are two main forms of vitamin K: K1 and K2. K1 helps with blood clotting, whereas K2 regulates calcium deposition (in other words, it promotes the calcification of bones and prevents the calcification of blood vessels and kidneys). Because of K2's role in calcium metabolism, it has an important role to play in bone health.

K2 is found in animal foods and fermented foods.

SO, WHAT'S MOST IMPORTANT?

Which nutrient do you think would be a potential issue for people on a plant-based diet? Most people would say calcium, because of the lack of dairy foods. This claim is certainly often made by the media, but it is false. Calcium is one of the most ubiquitous nutrients in our diet. If you are eating a wide array of plant foods – fruit, vegetables, nuts and seeds – you will be getting more than enough calcium.

In fact, it is vitamin D that could pose an issue for those on a plant-based diet, as the foods that contain the most vitamin D are animal foods. So, are plant-based diets bad for bone health? The truth is that, for anyone living in the northern hemisphere, regardless of diet, it is difficult to get enough vitamin D, because our main source is the sun. Therefore, taking a supplement is a must for everyone, but especially for those on a plant-based diet.

SKIN HEALTH

In truth, there isn't one particular diet that's best for skin health more than another, but there are key ingredients that are especially important. It just so happens that, all bar one, a plant-based diet is abundant in these, so many people who move over to a plant-based diet notice significant improvements in their skin's overall appearance.

These key nutrients help to keep skin healthy and can also influence the ageing of the skin.

FAT-SOLUBLE ANTIOXIDANTS

When it comes to skin health, you cannot move without hearing someone saying how wonderful antioxidants are for our skin, and how we should be consuming antioxidant-rich foods left, right and centre. Well, yes, that is a great idea for many reasons, but when it comes to the health of the skin, we need to get a little more specific.

There are literally thousands of chemicals found in our food chain that can have antioxidant activity, and their activity is as broad and as diverse as their number. They can have affinity for different body tissues, they act against different types of free radicals (unstable atoms that can damage cells) in different ways, they spend varying amounts of time in the body, and they are susceptible to degradation in different ways. However, antioxidants can be placed into two groups: water-soluble or fat-soluble. Water-soluble antioxidants, like vitamin C, for example, will deliver their activity within our systemic circulation and interstitial fluids (the fluid that bathes our cells). However, they have a limited lifespan and are quickly metabolized and excreted from the body. Fat-soluble antioxidants, on the other hand, are of particular importance when it comes to skin health.

Fat-soluble antioxidants, by their very nature, want to get out of the blood and into the fatty tissues – and they want to do it asap. Alongside dietary fats, they are absorbed into these fatty tissues via the lymphatics. Why is this relevant? Well, second to the brain, the most abundant fatty tissue in the body is the subcutaneous layer of the skin. So, these fat-soluble antioxidants can accumulate rapidly – and sometimes excessively – in this fatty layer.

Within the subcutaneous layer of the skin, we have many important structures; for example, the collagen and elastin matrix that gives skin its structural integrity. This protein lattice can be extremely susceptible to free-radical damage over time. Whether it is from excessive ultraviolet radiation exposure, pollution, smoking or excess drinking, free-radical damage to the collagen and elastin network can result in premature ageing of the skin, sagging and loss of plumpness and structural integrity.

Within this layer we also have the pilosebaceous unit, that structure where the sebaceous gland and hair follicle meet. This is the structure that becomes infected during an acne flare-up and is where the inflammation arises. Well, as we will see, some fat-soluble antioxidants can deliver localized anti-inflammatory activity that can help.

CAROTENOIDS

The carotenoids are a group of phytochemicals that are technically the plant form of vitamin A. They deliver yellow and orange colour pigments in foods. These are the absolute top of the list when it comes to fat-soluble antioxidants and skin health. This is because they rapidly migrate into the subcutaneous layer of the skin, where they can deliver antioxidant protection to the collagen and elastin matrix. They do this with such vigour that sometimes people who eat mainly raw foods, or who do a lot of juicing, can have an orangey tinge to their skin: a condition known as hypercarotenemia. This is testament to how effectively the carotenoids accumulate under the skin. This accumulation means they are on hand to deliver localized antioxidant support, especially upon exposure to UV.

The carotenoids also deliver some fairly potent anti-inflammatory activity. Inflammation is a key component of skin issues like acne and eczema, and these substances will be on hand to provide localized anti-inflammatory support.

Sweet potato, carrots, spinach and kale are all good sources of carotenoids.

VITAMIN E (TOCOPHEROLS AND TOCOTRIENOLS)

The second fat-soluble antioxidant of note is vitamin E. Like carotenoids, vitamin E can support the collagen and elastin fibres and protect them against free-radical damage, as well as protecting the skin cell membranes. Find this vitamin in almonds, hazelnuts, sunflower seeds and avocado.

WATER-SOLUBLE ANTIOXIDANTS

VITAMIN C

In a healthy wholefood, plant-based diet made up of a wide variety of fruit and vegetables, vitamin C will be naturally abundant. This water-soluble nutrient is best known for its role in immunity, as it can help white blood cells deliver certain toxic responses to pathogens or infected cells, as well as helping cells to move to the sight of infection faster. But vitamin C is also essential for the production of collagen. Vitamin C stimulates its production by influencing collagen mRNA, allowing production to be increased according to demand.

Collagen is one of the most important factors to consider if we care about how well we age, on the outside at least. This criss-cross lattice of protein helps to give skin its structural integrity. Think of it as a bit like the framework that your skin is bolted on to. You want that framework to be strong and well-maintained in order for your skin to stay wrinkle-free for as long as possible.

Peppers, broccoli, Brussels sprouts, papaya and oranges are all great sources of vitamin C.

ZINC

Providing your plant-based diet contains plenty of nuts and seeds, you should be getting enough zinc. It's a vital nutrient for the health of our skin. Firstly, zinc supports the immune system. Think about acne, the common and very distressing skin condition which I used to suffer from, and which was responsible for me discovering the power of nutrition. Acne is an active infection and a healthy immune response is necessary to keep it under control.

Zinc is used by our white blood cells to manufacture genes that control the way in which these cells respond to pathogens and do their job.

The second reason that zinc is so important to our skin is that it can regulate the activity of our sebaceous glands, which are the glands that produce oil in the skin. If the skin is too oily, zinc can help to reduce oil production. Likewise, if the skin is too dry, zinc can ramp up oil secretion.

OMEGA-3 FATTY ACIDS

These are the ones to watch if you're eating a plant-based diet. One of the most important groups of nutrients for healthy skin are the omega-3 fatty acids, and as you have seen throughout this opening section, plant-based diets fall very short in this area. Sure, you can get a form of omega 3 called ALA which is found in nuts and seeds, but this does very little in the body. It is the long-chain EPA and DHA (found in particularly high amounts in oily fish) which affect our physiology, and ALA from plants needs to go through significant chemical conversion to be turned into EPA and DHA. Humans are generally very poor at doing this conversion, leaving a plant-based diet inadequate (see pages 19–20).

Why are omega-3 fatty acids so important in skin health?

Anti-inflammatory action

Omega-3 fatty acids are one of the most important tools that we have at our disposal for the treatment of any type of inflammatory issue. When we process and metabolize dietary fats, one of the major metabolic end products is a group of communication molecules known as prostaglandins. One of the main roles of prostaglandins is to regulate different aspects of the inflammatory response.

There are three types of prostaglandin: series 1, series 2 and series 3. Series 1 and series 3 are involved in dampening down and deactivating the inflammatory response. Series 2 prostaglandins, in contrast, are involved in the instigation of the inflammatory response, and can make any currently active inflammation worse.

The type of prostaglandins produced will depend on the type of dietary fat that is consumed. Saturated animal fats, for example, are very high in a fatty acid called arachidonic acid, which, when metabolized, causes a rise in series 2 prostaglandins – the ones responsible for exacerbating inflammation. A diet high in omega-3 fatty acids, however, will cause an increase in the production of series 1 and series 3 prostaglandins – the ones that tackle inflammation. So, in essence, manipulating our dietary fat intake can directly influence the inflammatory response in the body.

Remember that virtually all skin lesions involve inflammation. The red, itchy flare-ups of eczema and the painful swelling of acne are both signs of active inflammation. So, anything we can do to make this less severe is hugely important.

Monounsaturated omega 9 also has an anti-inflammatory action in the body. Oleic acid, an omega-9 fatty acid, can be found in many healthy high-fat foods, such as olive oil, avocado and macadamia nuts.

Cell membrane health

Every cell in our body has a fatty membrane that gives the cell its shape and keeps the cell contents in while keeping toxins and pathogens out. Cell membranes are made up of a double layer of a fatty substance called phospholipids. The cell membranes also house a whole array of different receptors and transporters. These complex and highly organized structures allow interactions between the inner workings of the cell and its outer environment. They allow hormones to bind to the cell and instigate changes to the way in which the cell behaves. They allow nutrients to successfully enter the cell and for waste material to be removed. A healthy membrane means a healthy cell, which means healthy tissues.

Cell membranes require a constant stream of fatty acids in order to be able to constantly maintain themselves, to ensure that they remain soft, supple and strong, and that their many receptor sites remain fully functional. As you have probably guessed by now, the fats required for this maintenance are the omega-3 fatty acids.

If the membranes of skin cells are working optimally, the skin as an organ will function much better. There will be better oxygen delivery, better transport of nutrients to the area, and the skin's ability to retain moisture will be greatly improved. There is another added plus point. As the skin starts to work better, the effects of any topical products that we use, such as moisturizers and face masks, will be greatly enhanced.

GLOSSARY OF COMMON PHYTOCHEMICALS

The important thing to clarify here is that there are thousands of phytochemicals, each with their own specific activities, so what I have done is try to discuss the larger families of phytochemicals and give a broader view of their activities. If I went into detail on all of them, this would be one enormous – and probably very boring – book. I have included this brief glossary to prove a point more than anything, really – that plants deliver an extra powerful punch beyond just their nutrients.

BETALAINS

Betalains are nitrogen-containing water-soluble pigments with colours that range from yellow to reddish-violet. They are found in a variety of foods that are reddish in hue, and occur in red plants that do not contain anthocyanin molecules (flavonoids) as the red pigment (that is, beetroot contains betalains, whereas strawberries contain anthocyanins). They can be divided into two main subgroups: betaxanthins and betacyanins.

Betalains can have promising anti-inflammatory and antioxidant effects.

Common betalains
- Betacyanins
- Betaxanthins

How can they benefit us?
- Cardiovascular health
- Digestive health

Where you'll find them
- Beetroots
- Rainbow chard
- Amaranth
- Cactus fruits

CAROTENOIDS

Carotenoids are a very broadly distributed group of phytochemicals. They are primarily colour pigments in plants, found in the chloroplast of plant cells. In the body, carotenoids deliver mostly antioxidant activity. They are fat-soluble compounds, so they can accumulate in fatty tissues, such as the subcutaneous layer of the skin. When these compounds accumulate in the skin, they can offer a localized protection to the surrounding structures, such as collagen and elastin fibres and the pilosebaceous unit. This can essentially have an anti-ageing effect on your skin.

Carotenoids also have an anti-inflammatory activity. This is great for issues such as eczema, acne and psoriasis, which all involve redness and inflammation. They are also useful for inflammatory issues of the digestive tract.

In addition, carotenoids have a reputation for benefiting eye and prostate health. Lutein, a yellow-coloured carotenoid found in corn, orange peppers and squash, as well as broccoli and kale, can accumulate in the macula densa of the eye, and offer some protection against macular degeneration. The carotenoid lycopene, found in tomatoes, is believed to offer protection against prostate issues, such as prostatic hyperplasia and even prostate cancer. While there is debate around this, epidemiological data certainly does show an association between tomato intake and reduced prostate cancer risk. However, direct cause-and-effect relationships are yet to be confirmed.

Common carotenoids

- Alpha-carotene
- Beta-carotene
- Beta-cryptoxanthin
- Lutein
- Lycopene
- Zeaxanthin

How can they benefit us?

- Skin health
- Reducing skin ageing
- Reducing acne
- Reducing eczema
- Reducing psoriasis

Where you'll find them

- Carrots
- Tomatoes
- Mangos
- Melons
- Peppers
- Spinach

GLUCOSINOLATES

Glucosinolates are compounds commonly found in cruciferous vegetables that are becoming the focus of a great deal of research. They are made from glucose and amino acids, and are responsible for the bitter taste in foods such as Brussels sprouts and kale. Recent research has revealed that glucosinolates can cause a powerful stimulation of liver enzymes. These are the enzymes that can break down metabolic wastes, and also disarm potential carcinogens. There is also some evidence to suggest that glucosinolates can induce apoptosis (programmed cell death) in tumour cells.

Common glucosinolates
- Allicin
- Glucobrassicin
- Glucoraphanin
- Indole-3-carbinol
- Sulforaphane

How can they benefit us?
- Cellular health and wellbeing
- Hormone health
- Detoxification

Where you'll find them
- Broccoli
- Cauliflower
- Kale
- Brussels sprouts

POLYPHENOLS

Polyphenols are phytochemicals, and can be colour pigments, plant hormones or structural components.

Flavonoids

Flavonoids are the largest family of polyphenols. There are over 6,000 flavonoids, making them one of the most ubiquitous substances in our diets. They are mostly responsible for colour pigments in plants, predominantly shades of red, yellow and orange. They are a widely studied and powerful group of compounds with a very wide range of health benefits. Probably the best example of their protective activity is in cardiovascular health. They are known to protect blood vessels from damage, reduce cholesterol oxidation, lower blood pressure and reduce clotting factors. They also deliver antioxidant and anti-inflammatory effects.

Many flavonoids have a wide array of protective functions against some serious health conditions. They are known to influence various cell-signalling pathways, and this has been suggested as one of the ways in which flavonoids can improve cognitive function and even offer some protection against some forms of cancer.

Flavonoids also stimulate the activity of enzymes within our cells that are responsible for 'housekeeping'. They break down and remove certain toxins and metabolic waste products, keeping cells healthy.

Common flavonoids
- Anthocyanins
- Flavanols
- Flavanones
- Flavonols
- Flavones
- Isoflavones
- Quercetin
- Rutin

How can they benefit us?
- Heart health
- Cognitive function
- Reducing cholesterol
- Reducing blood pressure

Where you'll find them
- Red onions
- Red peppers
- Red wine
- Strawberries
- Raspberries
- Cabbage
- Green tea

Lignans

Lignans are also part of the polyphenol family. They are compounds that are found in certain seeds, such as flax and sesame. They are another phytochemical group that has been subject to considerable research, but has also been the subject of a wide array of hefty and sometimes dubious claims. One area where they do seem to shine is in supporting cardiovascular health, especially healthy cholesterol ratios. The balance between LDL and HDL, while hotly debated, does appear to remain a focal point for patients at risk of cardiovascular disease.

Lignans also seem to have an interesting effect on hormones. In women, they can bind to oestrogen receptors and selectively instigate an oestrogenic (having a similar effect to oestrogen in the body) or oestrogen-blocking activity. They also act on enzymes involved in oestrogen metabolism. In men, lignans appear to be able to prevent the conversion of testosterone into dihydrotestosterone, which can be a driver of prostatic diseases.

Common lignans
- Lariciresinol
- Matairesinol
- Pinoresinol
- Secoisolariciresinol

How can they benefit us?
- Improve HDL/LDL cholesterol levels
- Improve hormone levels in both men and women

Where you'll find them
- Flaxseeds
- Sesame seeds

THE RECIPES

DIGESTIVE HEALTH

CARDIOVASCULAR HEALTH

IMMUNE HEALTH

SKELETAL HEALTH

SKIN HEALTH

1 RAW

One thing is absolutely certain: the more raw fruit and vegetables we eat, the better. While there are some very, very daft claims in support of a 100 per cent raw food diet (which can be fine if done right, but let's just stick to the science), it is an absolute no-brainer to include as many raw, minimally processed plant foods in your diet as possible.

Many important micronutrients, such as vitamin C and the B vitamins, are both water-soluble and heat-sensitive, so are easily damaged by cooking. Many of the more delicate antioxidants, too, are easily damaged by heat, so eating plenty of raw foods is definitely worth doing.

Fibre
Flavonoids
Vitamin C

**SERVES: 4 AS A SIDE OR
2 AS A MAIN COURSE**
1 fennel bulb, sliced
  lengthways
1 orange, segments separated
Large handful of baby spinach
Black pepper, to taste

For the dressing
1 teaspoon English mustard
1 teaspoon maple syrup
1 teaspoon toasted sesame oil
2 teaspoons olive oil

This fresh, zingy salad makes a great accompaniment to almost any dish. It also works well as a main course for a light lunch.

FENNEL AND ORANGE SALAD

In a bowl, combine the fennel slices, orange segments and spinach.

In a separate bowl, whisk together all the dressing ingredients, then dress the salad before serving, seasoned with a little black pepper.

Beta-carotene
Calcium
Glucosinolates
Magnesium
Potassium
Vitamin K

SERVES: 4

250g (9oz) curly kale,
    tough stalks removed
Olive oil, for drizzling
1 large garlic clove,
    finely chopped
1 small red chilli, deseeded
    and finely chopped
2 tablespoons almond butter
2 teaspoons soy sauce
2 teaspoons maple syrup
Juice of ½ lime
Small coriander sprig,
    chopped, to garnish
Salt

I absolutely adore this recipe. The flavours and nutrient density are off the charts. As this is so filling, you may find that just a big bowlful on its own can keep you going for hours. Massaging raw kale softens it and makes it easier to digest.

KALE SALAD WITH ALMOND CHILLI SAUCE

Place the kale in a bowl. Drizzle over a little olive oil and sprinkle over some salt, then massage the kale with your hands for about 30 seconds.

In a separate small bowl, thoroughly mix together the garlic, chilli, almond butter, soy sauce, maple syrup and lime juice. If the sauce is too thick, add a splash of water to thin it out.

Drizzle the sauce over the massaged kale, garnish with coriander and serve.

Beta-carotene
Flavonoids
Magnesium
Vitamin C

SERVES: 2
8 large lettuce leaves
   (any variety will do)
½ red onion, thinly sliced
½ cucumber, thinly sliced
1 ripe mango, thinly sliced
1 small bunch of coriander,
   leaves picked
1 small chilli, deseeded
   and thinly sliced

For the dipping sauce
1 teaspoon white wine vinegar
2 teaspoons toasted sesame oil
1 tablespoon pineapple juice
1 garlic clove, crushed

Lettuce wraps are a raw-food staple. This is build-it-yourself plant-based food at its best.

MANGO, CHILLI AND CORIANDER LETTUCE WRAPS

In a small bowl, mix the dipping sauce ingredients together and whisk well. The oil and the juice will separate, but just give it a little stir each time you dip.

Place the lettuce leaves on a plate and fill each one with a combination of all the other remaining ingredients, then roll them up, dip and enjoy!

**SERVES: 4 AS A SIDE OR
2 AS A MAIN COURSE**

400g (14oz) can chickpeas,
   drained
5cm (2in) piece of cucumber,
   cut into small dice
½ red onion, finely chopped
3–4 plum tomatoes,
   finely chopped
Small handful of baby
   spinach, shredded
½ small red chilli, deseeded
   and finely chopped
Small bunch of coriander,
   roughly chopped
½ teaspoon smoked
   sweet paprika
¼ teaspoon garlic salt
Black pepper, to taste

*This flavoursome little salad is lovely and filling
because it uses chickpeas as a base. It's ideal
as a main course and makes a great lunch.*

CHICKPEA CHOPPED SALAD

Place all the ingredients in a bowl and toss together
to make sure everything is mixed well and coated
in all the flavours.

Season with a little black pepper and serve.

This is another filling salad that's perfect as a main course. When I spent a fair bit of time in Mexico City, I came to love the simple yet vibrant flavours of the traditional dishes served there. Here, I've recreated those distinctive Mexican flavours.

RICH IN:
Anthocyanins
Lutein
Oleic acid
Vitamin E

SERVES: 4
400g (14oz) can black beans, drained
200g (7oz) can sweetcorn, drained
2–3 tablespoons jarred jalapeños, roughly chopped, plus 1 tablespoon juice from the jar
1 ripe avocado, cut into small dice
1 large red onion, finely chopped
1 bunch of coriander, leaves roughly chopped
Juice of 1 lime
1 tablespoon extra virgin olive oil

BLACK BEAN, CORN, JALAPEÑO, AVOCADO AND RED ONION SALAD

Combine all the ingredients in a bowl and toss together well.

Serve immediately.

Vegetable noodles have really become a 'thing' in recent years, so much so that you can now buy them in supermarkets ready prepared. They are the staple of raw-food faddists and seem to require all sorts of gadgets to create them. However, if you don't have one, a simple peeler will do the trick.

RICH IN:
Beta-carotene
Magnesium
Oleic acid
Vitamin E

SERVES: 4 AS A SIDE OR 2 AS A MAIN COURSE
1 large courgette
2 large carrots

For the dressing
1 small bunch of coriander
1 small bunch of flat-leaf parsley
1 teaspoon capers
5 pitted green olives
1 large garlic clove, finely chopped
1 teaspoon white wine vinegar
1 tablespoon olive oil
½ ripe avocado
Salt, to taste

COURGETTE AND CARROT NOODLES WITH GREEN HERB DRESSING

Place the dressing ingredients in a blender and blend into a smooth, creamy dressing.

Using a vegetable peeler, or a spiralizer if you have one, create noodles from the courgette and carrots. If you're using a peeler, simply run it gently along the length of the vegetable to create a thin, flat noodle.

Combine the noodles in a bowl, pour the dressing over the top and toss before serving.

I absolutely adore Korean food and bibimbap is one of my favourite Korean dishes. This is an interesting twist on the popular dish. While the gochujang (Korean chilli paste) isn't strictly raw, the core ingredients are – and, anyway, who cares when it tastes this amazing and does you so much good?! If you can't find gochujang, sriracha can work as a substitute.

RICH IN:
Beta-carotene
Glucosinolates
Inulin
Magnesium

SERVES: 2
1 large cauliflower
½ red onion, thinly sliced
3 handfuls of baby spinach, thinly shredded
1 large carrot, grated or shredded
2–3 spring onions, cut into matchsticks
2 heaped tablespoons gochujang
6 teaspoons toasted sesame oil
2 tablespoons lime juice

CAULIFLOWER 'RICE' BIBIMBAP

Separate the cauliflower into small florets and place these in a food processor. Pulse until the cauliflower is finely chopped and resembles rice.

Tip the cauliflower 'rice' into a serving bowl, then add the red onion, spinach, carrot and spring onions.

Whisk together the gochujang, sesame oil and lime juice. Drizzle the dressing over the vegetables and mix well before serving.

Kelp noodles are quite similar to glass noodles, but are made from seaweed. They're actually raw and just need to be rehydrated in water. They take on flavour really well and have a lovely texture.

KELP NOODLE SALAD WITH MISO SESAME DRESSING

SERVES: 4
350g (12oz) kelp or
    konjac noodles
1 large carrot, cut into fine
    matchsticks (or use a
    julienne peeler)
3 spring onions, shredded
1 courgette, cut into
    matchsticks
1 small bunch of coriander

For the dressing
1 tablespoon white miso paste
2 teaspoons maple syrup
1 teaspoon white wine vinegar
2 teaspoons water

Hydrate the kelp noodles according to the packet instructions, then place the hydrated noodles in a bowl and add the vegetables. Toss well so they are evenly mixed.

In a small bowl or jug, mix together the dressing ingredients, adding a little more water to make it pourable, if needed.

Pour the dressing over the noodles and toss well to ensure everything is fully coated, then serve.

2 BLITZ AND BLEND

The blender is one of the greatest tools for getting the best out of a wholefood, plant-based diet. Whether it is for convenience – such as knocking up a quick soup – or as a way to bring different textures to your meals (you will see a fair few purées featuring in the Time on Your Hands chapter, for example), your blender will become your best friend.

Kitting yourself out with a decent blender and/or food processor will help you to bring a wholefood, plant-based diet to life. Make sure you get one with a lot of power, if possible, to break down all those vegetable fibres.

This simple soup is packed to the hilt with flavour. You could really throw together any vegetables here, but this classic combo works the best, in my opinion.

ROASTED TOMATO AND RED PEPPER SOUP

SERVES: 4

1 large red onion,
   finely chopped
3 garlic cloves,
   finely chopped
2 large red peppers,
   cored, deseeded
   and chopped
5–6 large plum tomatoes,
   quartered
Olive oil, for drizzling
200–300ml (7–10fl oz)
   vegetable stock
Salt and black pepper

For the garnish (optional)
Handful of basil
Pinch of red chilli flakes

Preheat the oven to 200°C (400°F), Gas Mark 6.

Place the onion, garlic, red peppers and tomatoes in a roasting tin and drizzle with a little olive oil. Season with salt and black pepper and toss together well.

Roast for about 30 minutes until all the ingredients have softened. Make sure you stir everything a couple of times during roasting. The tomatoes will break down a great deal in this process, creating a rich sauce.

Transfer the roasted veg to a blender and add enough stock to come halfway up the ingredients. Blend until smooth. Serve immediately, garnished with basil and red chilli flakes, if using.

I absolutely love black beans, and they pack quite the nutritional punch. Their 'black' colour is actually a deep purple delivered by those powerful flavonoids. No other beans have their antioxidant levels and cardioprotective capacity, so get 'em in!

RICH IN:
Fibre
Flavonoids
Oligosaccharides

SERVES: 4
1 large red onion,
    finely chopped
3 garlic cloves,
    finely chopped
Olive oil, for sautéing
    (optional), plus extra
    for drizzling
1 large potato, diced
400g (14oz) can black
    beans, drained
400ml (14fl oz) vegetable
    stock (you may not
    need all of this)
1 teaspoon medium
    curry powder

For the garnish (optional)
Chopped red chilli
Black pepper, to taste

CURRIED BLACK BEAN SOUP

In a saucepan over a medium heat, sauté the onion and garlic in a little olive oil (or water), along with a good pinch of salt, for about 10 minutes until softened.

Add the potato and black beans and enough vegetable stock to almost cover the ingredients. Simmer for 15 minutes until the potato has softened.

Transfer the mixture to a blender, add the curry powder and blitz until smooth. (If you prefer, you can use a stick blender.) Serve immediately, garnished with a drizzle of olive oil, and some chopped red chilli and black pepper, if using.

SERVES: 4
1 large red onion,
  finely chopped
2 garlic cloves,
  finely chopped
Olive oil, for sautéing
400g (14oz) carrots, chopped
Juice of 2 large oranges
400ml (14fl oz) vegetable
  stock (you may not
  need all of this)
1 teaspoon caraway seeds
Black pepper, to garnish

Carrot and orange is a classic flavour combination that never fails to satisfy. If you don't have any caraway seeds, you could try fennel seeds instead.

CARROT, ORANGE AND CARAWAY SOUP

In a saucepan over a medium heat, sauté the onion and garlic in a little olive oil, along with a good pinch of salt, for about 10 minutes until softened.

Add the carrots, orange juice and enough stock to almost cover the carrots.

Simmer for 15 minutes until the carrots have softened. Transfer to a blender (or use a stick blender) and blitz until smooth.

Stir in the caraway seeds before serving, garnished with black pepper.

SERVES: 2–3
1 large red onion,
  finely chopped
2 garlic cloves,
  finely chopped
1 large red pepper, cored,
  deseeded and diced
4 large tomatoes,
  roughly chopped
500g (18oz) passata
200ml (7fl oz) vegetable stock
4 tablespoons olive oil, plus
  1 tablespoon for drizzling
1 tablespoon red wine vinegar
1 teaspoon hot sauce
5cm (2in) piece of cucumber,
  chopped into small dice,
  to garnish
Black pepper, to taste

I have to admit, it took me a little while to get my head around gazpacho. A cold, raw soup! But once I actually gave it a go, I soon grew to love it. It's perfect for a family get-together on a hot day. You could leave out the olive oil if you're following a low-oil plan; just add an additional 100g (3½oz) passata.

GORGEOUS GAZPACHO

Place all the ingredients in your blender and blitz until as smooth as possible. A little bit of texture is okay, but the smoother the better, generally. Chill in the refrigerator for at least 4 hours.

Serve garnished with diced cucumber and black pepper and drizzled with the remaining olive oil.

This is an absolute belter: smooth, creamy and a little bit fiery. It's a great soup for the winter, but can also be a delicious base for a curry if you have leftovers.

RICH IN:
Beta-carotene
B vitamins
Fibre
Iron
Oligosaccharides

SERVES: 4
1 large red onion,
    finely chopped
3 large garlic cloves,
    finely chopped
5cm (2in) piece of ginger,
    peeled and finely chopped
Olive oil, for sautéing
2 large sweet potatoes,
    peeled and diced
350g (12oz) dried red lentils
400ml (14fl oz) can
    coconut milk
400ml (14fl oz) vegetable
    stock (you may not
    need all of this)
Salt

SWEET POTATO, RED LENTIL, COCONUT AND GINGER SOUP

In a saucepan over a medium heat, sauté the red onion, garlic and ginger in a little olive oil, along with a good pinch of salt, for about 10 minutes until softened.

Add the diced sweet potatoes, red lentils, coconut milk and enough vegetable stock to almost cover the contents of the pan. Simmer for about 20 minutes until both the potatoes and lentils have softened, and the lentils are beginning to break down. You may need to add small amounts of extra stock during this stage if the pan is looking a little dry.

Transfer the mixture to a blender (or use a stick blender) and blitz until smooth. Serve immediately.

SERVES: 4
280g (10oz) jar artichoke
   hearts, drained
200g (7oz) pitted green
   olives, drained
1 garlic clove,
   finely chopped
2 tablespoons extra
   virgin olive oil

This is a mouth-watering spread that is ridiculously simple but ridiculously tasty. It's great on crostinis and jacket potatoes, as a sandwich filler or as a simple dip.

OLIVE AND ARTICHOKE SPREAD

Place all the ingredients in a blender and blitz into a coarse purée.

Serve immediately.

This is something a little different, but it absolutely hits the spot. If you have never combined beetroot and wasabi before, you won't regret it. The earthiness and heat blend beautifully.

RICH IN:
Betacyanin
Calcium
Iron
Potassium

SERVES: 4
50g (1¾oz) walnuts
200g (7oz) cooked beetroot
   (not the pickled variety)
1½ tablespoons tahini
1 garlic clove, finely chopped
1 heaped teaspoon wasabi
4 tablespoons lemon juice
Grilled flatbreads, to serve

BEETROOT, WALNUT AND WASABI DIP

Place all the ingredients in a food processor or blender, reserving a few walnuts, and blitz into a rough-textured dip.

Chop the remaining walnuts into small pieces and sprinkle them over the dip to garnish. Serve with grilled flatbreads.

This is a beautiful raw dip that has a spectacular flavour. It makes the perfect snack spread on oatcakes and tastes incredible on toast.

RICH IN:
Lycopene
Oleic acid
Vitamin C
Vitamin E
Vitamin K

SERVES: 4
1 large, very ripe avocado
8 sun-dried tomatoes (the variety in oil works best)
25g (1oz) basil leaves
3 tablespoons extra virgin olive oil (optional)

AVOCADO, SUN-DRIED TOMATO AND BASIL DIP

Scoop the avocado flesh into a blender or a food processor.

Add the remaining ingredients and blitz to a coarse purée.

RICH IN:
Beta-carotene
B vitamins
Calcium
Fibre
Iron
Magnesium

SERVES: 4
6–7 carrots, sliced lengthways
Olive oil, for roasting
150g (5½oz) dried red lentils
2 tablespoons coconut yogurt
1 garlic clove, finely chopped
½ teaspoon ground cumin
Salt and black pepper
Coriander leaves, to garnish

This is a gorgeous dip or spread that is perfect with oatcakes, spread on toast or in a wrap with some roasted cauliflower.

RED LENTIL AND ROASTED CARROT DIP

Preheat the oven to 200°C (400°F), Gas Mark 6.

Place the carrots in a roasting tin, drizzle with a small amount of olive oil and roast for 25–30 minutes, or until softened and golden brown.

While the carrots are cooking, place the lentils in a saucepan over a medium heat, cover with hot water, bring up to a simmer and cook for 20 minutes until soft, then drain.

Place the roasted carrots, cooked lentils, coconut yogurt, garlic and cumin in a food processor or blender and blitz until quite smooth.

Season well and allow to cool. Garnish with the coriander leaves before serving.

This really is a flavour explosion. It makes a delicious sandwich filler and works well with some watercress or baby spinach and fresh tomatoes.

RICH IN:
B vitamins
Immunomodulatory polysaccharides
Isoflavones
Vitamin K

SERVES: 4
300g (10½oz) chestnut
  mushrooms, sliced
  or quartered
½ red onion, thinly sliced
1 garlic clove, finely chopped
Olive oil, for roasting
1 heaped tablespoon
  brown miso paste
Black pepper, to taste

ROASTED MUSHROOM AND MISO SANDWICH FILLER

Preheat the oven to 200°C (400°F), Gas Mark 6.

Place the mushrooms, onion and garlic in a roasting tin, drizzle with a small amount of olive oil and roast for around 30 minutes or until the mushrooms and onion have softened.

Transfer to a blender or food processor, along with any liquid at the bottom of the tin.

Add the miso paste and blitz until smooth.

RICH IN:
B vitamins
Calcium
Isoflavones
Magnesium
Soluble fibre
Vitamin C

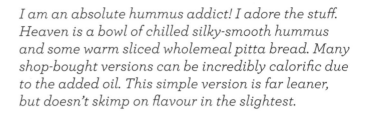

SERVES: 4
400g (14oz) can
   chickpeas, drained,
   but liquid reserved
1 tablespoon tahini
8 tablespoons lemon juice
1 large garlic clove,
   finely chopped
Salt

I am an absolute hummus addict! I adore the stuff. Heaven is a bowl of chilled silky-smooth hummus and some warm sliced wholemeal pitta bread. Many shop-bought versions can be incredibly calorific due to the added oil. This simple version is far leaner, but doesn't skimp on flavour in the slightest.

A LEAN CLASSIC HUMMUS

Place the chickpeas, tahini, lemon juice and garlic in a food processor or blender, along with a generous pinch of salt, and blend. It will have quite a thick texture at this stage. Begin adding the chickpea liquid in small increments until you get a luscious, creamy texture.

Chill for 3–4 hours before serving.

RICH IN:
Beta-carotene
B vitamins
Iron
Oligosaccharides
Vitamin C

SERVES: 4
1 large red pepper, cored,
    deseeded and sliced
Olive oil, for roasting
400g (14oz) can cannellini
    beans, drained
1 large garlic clove,
    finely chopped
Salt

This is kind of like hummus 2.0. The super-smooth and creamy texture from the puréed cannellini beans is absolutely divine, and they match so well with roasted red peppers. This dip is great on sweet potato wedges or with vegetable crudités.

CANNELLINI BEAN AND ROASTED PEPPER DIP

Preheat the oven to 200°C (400°F), Gas Mark 6.

Spread out the sliced pepper on a baking tray, drizzle with a small amount of olive oil and toss. Roast for around 25 minutes, or until softened and starting to char at the edges.

Place the roasted peppers, cannellini beans and garlic in a food processor or blender and blitz to form a smooth paste.

Season well with salt and allow to cool before serving.

3 STOVE TOP

I almost called this chapter 'one-pot wonders',
as most of these dishes really are very much that.
Throw everything into one big pot and they mostly
look after themselves. There are a few, though, that
require a bit more work. The beauty of these recipes
is that they illustrate just how simple preparing
good, healthy food really is.

RICH IN:
B vitamins
Carotenoids
Magnesium
Vitamin C
Vitamin E

This is one-pot magic at its very best. So many people are put off making curries from scratch, believing that they are overly complex. Sure, some can be, but this one is not only beginner friendly – it also tastes out of this world!

NUTTY SWEET POTATO AND SPINACH CURRY

SERVES: 4

1 large red onion, chopped
4 garlic cloves, finely chopped
1 red chilli, deseeded and finely chopped
Thumb-sized piece of fresh root ginger, peeled and finely chopped
Olive oil, for sautéing
1 teaspoon ground cumin
1 teaspoon ground coriander
1 teaspoon garam masala
1 teaspoon ground turmeric
½ teaspoon ground cinnamon
2–3 sweet potatoes, skin on, diced
500ml (18fl oz) vegetable stock (you may not need all of this)
1 heaped tablespoon crunchy peanut butter
4 handfuls of baby spinach
Salt

In a large, heavy-based saucepan over a medium heat, sauté the onion, garlic, chilli and ginger in a little olive oil, along with a good pinch of salt, for about 10 minutes until softened.

Add the cumin, coriander, garam masala, turmeric and cinnamon, and sauté for a further 2–3 minutes until aromatic.

Add the diced sweet potatoes and enough vegetable stock to cover the contents of the pan by about two-thirds. Simmer over a medium heat for 30–45 minutes, stirring often, until the liquid has reduced right down and the starch has leached from the sweet potatoes to create a thick sauce. This may seem like it is taking a while, but be patient.

Once the sauce has thickened, add the peanut butter and stir. Take the pan off the heat and stir in the spinach until it wilts, then serve.

This dish is just gorgeous – indulgent, flavoursome, nutrient-dense. I am using the classic basil for this pesto, but you could throw in any fresh herbs and really jazz it up.

RICH IN:
Magnesium
Oleic Acid
Vitamin E
Zinc

SERVES: 4
300g (10½oz) wholewheat
    penne pasta
1 large red onion, sliced
1 large courgette,
    cut into half circles
Olive oil, for sautéing
4 large handfuls of
    baby spinach
Salt

For the walnut pesto
50g (1¾oz) walnuts,
    roughly chopped
1 teaspoon pine nuts
Large bunch of basil,
    roughly chopped
1 large garlic clove,
    finely chopped
2 tablespoons
    nutritional yeast
150ml (5fl oz) olive oil

PENNE WITH COURGETTES, SPINACH AND WALNUT PESTO

Add the pasta to a pan of salted boiling water. Cook, according to the packet instructions, until al dente. Drain and set aside.

In a heavy-based saucepan over a medium heat, sauté the red onion and courgette in a small amount of olive oil, along with a good pinch of salt, for about 10 minutes until both have softened. Add the baby spinach at this point and sauté for a minute or so until wilted.

Make the pesto, either by placing all the ingredients in a pestle and mortar and grinding to a rough consistency, or by placing them in a food processor and blending on a fairly low setting. Pesto always seems to have more character when it has some texture.

Add the drained pasta to the vegetables and stir well.

Finally, add the pesto and stir through, ensuring everything is mixed well, then serve.

SERVES: 2–3

1 large red onion,
    finely chopped
3 garlic cloves,
    finely chopped
1 small red chilli,
    deseeded and
    finely chopped
Olive oil, for sautéing
1 large courgette,
    cut into half circles
3 handfuls of curly kale,
    tough stalks removed
2 × 400g (14oz) cans black
    beans, drained
300g (10oz) passata
1 tablespoon smoked
    sweet paprika, plus
    extra to garnish
2 teaspoons ground cumin
Salt and black pepper
Dairy-free yogurt, to serve

*This dish has a hearty, warming, comforting vibe.
It's great on a baked sweet potato or served with some
brown rice – or simply enjoy a big bowl of it by itself.*

BLACK BEAN, COURGETTE AND KALE CHILLI

In a large, heavy-based saucepan over a medium heat, sauté the onion, garlic and chilli in a little olive oil, along with a good pinch of salt, for about 10 minutes until softened.

Add the courgette and continue to sauté for 2–3 minutes, then add the kale and sauté for another 2 minutes.

Add the black beans, passata, paprika and cumin, and then season. Reduce the heat and simmer for 20 minutes, stirring regularly.

Taste and add more spices or seasoning, if necessary, before serving with a dollop of dairy-free yogurt, garnished with extra paprika.

SERVES: 4
1 large red onion,
   finely chopped
4 garlic cloves,
   finely chopped
Olive oil, for sautéing
2 teaspoons hot curry paste
1 teaspoon ground turmeric
300g (10½oz) dried red lentils
400g (14oz) can coconut milk
1 large sweet potato,
   peeled and diced
150g (5½oz) frozen peas
600ml (20fl oz) vegetable
   stock
Salt and black pepper

Comfort in a bowl, this is seriously filling and micronutrient-rich. I can happily eat this on its own – serving it with rice would be a bit of a carb overload.

SWEET POTATO AND COCONUT DHAL

In a large, heavy-based saucepan over a medium heat, sauté the onion and garlic in a little olive oil, along with a good pinch of salt, for about 10 minutes until softened.

Add the curry paste, turmeric, lentils and coconut milk, bring to a simmer and cook for 2–3 minutes.

Add the diced sweet potato. Begin adding the vegetable stock bit by bit, stirring often. When the stock has been absorbed, add a little more, and so on until the sweet potato has softened and the lentils have broken down. This should take around 20 minutes and the end texture should resemble porridge.

Add the frozen peas, then season and simmer for another 2–3 minutes until the peas are cooked.

Serve immediately.

B vitamins
Iron
Magnesium
Soluble fibre

SERVES: 4
1 large red onion,
    finely chopped
4 garlic cloves,
    finely chopped
2.5cm (1in) piece of fresh
    root ginger, peeled and
    finely chopped
Olive oil, for sautéing
300g (10½oz) dried red lentils
500ml (18fl oz) vegetable
    stock (you may not need
    all of this)
½ teaspoon ground cumin
1 heaped teaspoon mild
    curry powder
1 teaspoon ground turmeric
4 large handfuls of baby
    spinach
150g (5½oz) brown rice
Salt and black pepper

Who doesn't love a good dhal? My favourite of all dhals is a saag dhal, aka spinach dhal. This simple recipe is sure to be a winner. It's perfect served with brown rice or on baked sweet potatoes.

SPINACH DHAL

In a large saucepan over a medium heat, sauté the onion, garlic and ginger in a little olive oil, along with a good pinch of sea salt, for about 10 minutes until softened.

Add the lentils and then begin adding the stock, bit by bit, stirring often. When the stock has been absorbed, add a little more, and so on – as if you're making a risotto. This should take around 20 minutes and the end texture should resemble porridge.

Meanwhile, cook the rice in a large saucepan of boiling water according to the packet instructions.

Add the cumin, curry powder and turmeric to the lentil mixture, season and cook for a few minutes more.

Add the baby spinach and stir for a minute or so until it has wilted. Serve with the rice.

Calcium
Flavonoids
Immunomodulatory
polysaccharides
Inulin
Selenium

SERVES: 2
125g (4½oz) soba noodles
1 large red onion,
    finely chopped
3 garlic cloves, finely chopped
1 small red chilli, deseeded
    and finely chopped
Olive oil, for stir-frying
6 shiitake mushrooms, sliced
2 spring onions, sliced
    into batons
1 large courgette, cut into
    3cm (1in) matchsticks
2 handfuls of shredded spring
    greens or cabbage
100g (3½oz) firm tofu, diced
1 tablespoon maple syrup
1 tablespoon soy sauce
1 tablespoon sesame oil
2 teaspoons toasted sesame
    seeds, to garnish

Having spent a great deal of time in Asia, I am a huge fan of noodles in any form: fried noodles, soup noodles – love 'em all. This simple dish is the perfect combination of comfort food and lots of flavour.

SPICY SESAME MAPLE SOBA NOODLES

Begin by cooking the noodles. Simply place in a saucepan, cover with boiling water and simmer for around 10 minutes until soft. Drain and set aside.

In a wok or large, heavy-based frying pan over a medium heat, stir-fry the red onion, garlic and chilli in a little olive oil, along with a good pinch of salt, for about 10 minutes until softened.

Add the mushrooms, spring onions, courgette and shredded greens or cabbage and continue to stir-fry for 5 minutes.

Add the cooked noodles and tofu and mix everything together well.

Add the maple syrup, soy sauce and sesame oil, and mix well once again, ensuring everything is coated.

Divide between 2 plates and garnish with the toasted sesame seeds before serving.

B vitamins
Calcium
Immunomodulatory
polysaccharides
Isoflavones
Magnesium

SERVES: 2

2 tablespoons brown
    miso paste
750ml (1⅓ pints) water
5–6 shiitake mushrooms,
    sliced
100g (3½oz) firm tofu, cubed
2 tablespoons dried
    wakame seaweed
6 long-stem broccoli stems
125g (4½oz) soba noodles
    or thin rice noodles
3 spring onions, sliced,
    to garnish

On my many journeys around Japan, I have enjoyed some wonderful ramen, especially in Fukuoka, a city famous for its ramen. This filling yet light noodle soup can have a variety of different bases: meat/bone broth, dashi and, like this version, miso! Wakame can be found in health-food stores and some supermarkets, but if you can't get hold of it, try dulse instead.

RAMEN BOWLS

In a large saucepan over a medium heat, mix together the miso paste and the measured water and bring up to a gentle simmer.

Once the miso has dissolved, add the mushrooms, tofu, wakame and broccoli, then simmer for 5 minutes until the mushrooms and broccoli are cooked.

In a second saucepan, cook the noodles according to the packet instructions, then drain. Divide the cooked noodles between 2 large serving bowls. Spoon the vegetables and tofu over each portion, then pour over the soup base.

Garnish both bowls with the sliced spring onions before serving.

SERVES: 4
500g (1lb 2oz) vegan gnocchi
Large handful of baby spinach
Black pepper, to taste

For the cashew cream
150g (5½oz) cashew nuts
1 tablespoon lemon juice
120ml (4fl oz) water
Salt, to taste

For the tomato sauce
1 large red onion,
    finely chopped
3 garlic cloves, finely chopped
Olive oil, for sautéing
400g (14oz) can chopped
    tomatoes
4 tomatoes, quartered
½ teaspoon red chilli flakes,
    plus extra to garnish

This dish takes a bit of extra effort, but it is really worth it. You will need a high-powered blender, but if you don't have one, a shop-bought vegan cream alternative is a suitable replacement for the cashew cream.

CREAMY TOMATO AND CHILLI GNOCCHI

Start by making the cashew cream. Simply place all the ingredients in a high-powered blender and blend into a smooth cream.

Next, make the tomato sauce. In a heavy-based saucepan over a medium heat, sauté the onion and garlic in a little olive oil, along with a good pinch of salt, for about 10 minutes until softened.

Add the canned chopped tomatoes, fresh tomatoes and chilli flakes and simmer for around 15 minutes.

Meanwhile, place the gnocchi in a second saucepan and cover with boiling water. Simmer for a few minutes, or until all the gnocchi float to the top.

Pour the tomato sauce into the blender with the cashew cream and blend into a smooth, creamy sauce. Alternatively, you could use a stick blender.

When the gnocchi are cooked, drain, then tip back into the saucepan and pour over the sauce. Finally, add the spinach and stir through to wilt before serving, garnished with black pepper and red chilli flakes.

This is one of my lifelong favourites. I have been making it for years and it is always a crowd-pleaser. The best sun-dried tomatoes to use here are the dry variety, rather than the ones in oil, simply because they give more flavour to the final dish.

RICH IN:
Carotenoids
Vitamin C

SUN-DRIED TOMATO AND RED PEPPER RISOTTO

SERVES: 4

1 large red onion,
  finely chopped
3 garlic cloves,
  finely chopped
100g (3½oz) sun-dried
  tomatoes, sliced
Olive oil, for sautéing
250g (9oz) Arborio risotto rice
400g (14oz) can chopped
  tomatoes
1 litre (1¾ pints) vegetable
  stock (you may need a
  bit more or less)
2 large red peppers, cored,
  deseeded and diced
Salt and black pepper
Handful of basil, to garnish
  (optional)

In a heavy-based saucepan over a medium heat, sauté the onion, garlic and sun-dried tomatoes in a little olive oil, along with a good pinch of salt, for about 10 minutes until softened.

Add the risotto rice and the can of chopped tomatoes, bring to a simmer and cook for 7–8 minutes.

Start adding the vegetable stock, bit by bit, stirring often. The rice absorbs the stock fairly quickly, at which point you need to add a little more. Keep going until the rice is almost cooked and the risotto has a porridge-like texture. This should take around 40 minutes.

At this point, add the red peppers. Continue to cook for 10 minutes until the peppers have softened nicely, the remaining stock has reduced a little more and the risotto has a firm texture.

Garnish with basil leaves, if using, grind some black pepper on top, and serve.

RICH IN:
B vitamins
Iron
Lycopene
Soluble fibre
Zinc

SERVES: 2
1 large red onion,
   finely chopped
3 garlic cloves,
   finely chopped
Olive oil, for sautéing
½ red pepper, cored,
   deseeded and diced
400g (14oz) can Puy lentils
400g (14oz) can chopped
   tomatoes
1 tablespoon mixed
   herbs (optional)
2 teaspoons vegetable
   stock powder
2 handfuls of baby spinach
250g (9oz) wholewheat
   spaghetti
Salt and black pepper

This is a dish that is sure to become a firm family favourite. It is just so flavoursome and comforting.

SPAGHETTI WITH PUY LENTIL BOLOGNESE

In a large, heavy-based saucepan over a medium heat, sauté the onion and garlic in a little olive oil, along with a good pinch of salt, for 10 minutes until softened.

Add the red pepper and sauté for 5 minutes, then add the Puy lentils, chopped tomatoes and mixed herbs, if using, and simmer for 15 minutes.

Add the stock powder and simmer for another 10 minutes until the mixture has reduced and the lentils have broken down slightly. You want it to resemble a traditional beef Bolognese.

Meanwhile, add the spaghetti to a saucepan of salted boiling water. Cook, according to the packet instructions, until al dente. Drain and set aside.

Add the baby spinach to the Bolognese and stir through to wilt.

Add the pasta to the Bolognese sauce and toss to coat. Season to taste before serving.

SERVES: 4

1 large red onion,
    finely chopped
3 garlic cloves,
    finely chopped
Olive oil, for sautéing
1 courgette, cut into half circles
1 red pepper, cored, deseeded
    and roughly chopped
400g (14oz) can chopped
    tomatoes
400g (14oz) can chickpeas,
    drained
2 tablespoons pitted green
    olives
6 dried apricots, cut into
    small pieces
2 teaspoons ground cinnamon
1 teaspoon za'atar
½ teaspoon ground turmeric
120g (4½oz) wholewheat
    couscous
175ml (6fl oz) boiling water
2 handfuls of baby spinach
Salt and black pepper

This is a lovely dish that is really just a nod to the flavours of Morocco, rather than being a traditional recipe. Flavoursome and moreish.

MOROCCAN-STYLE VEGETABLE STEW

In a large saucepan over a medium heat, sauté the red onion and garlic in a little olive oil, along with a good pinch of salt, for about 10 minutes until softened.

Add the courgette and pepper and sauté for another 5 minutes.

Add the chopped tomatoes, chickpeas, olives and apricots, and simmer for 10 minutes.

Add the cinnamon, za'atar and turmeric, season, and simmer for another 15–20 minutes, stirring well. You want to get to the stage where the sauce has thickened and darkened and the flavours have intensified. You can always stew it for a little longer, if you want to.

Meanwhile, place the couscous in a bowl, add the boiling water and cover for 10 minutes. Fluff up with a fork.

Finally add the baby spinach to the stew and allow it to wilt as you stir it in.

Divide the couscous and stew between 4 bowls and serve immediately.

SERVES: 2
1 large red onion,
  halved and sliced
2 garlic cloves,
  finely chopped
Olive oil, for sautéing
1 large aubergine, diced
1 large courgette, diced
3–4 large tomatoes, quartered
1 heaped tablespoon capers
2 tablespoons pitted green
  or black olives
200ml (7fl oz) canned
  chopped tomatoes
2 tablespoons red
  wine vinegar
1 teaspoon dried mixed herbs
120g (4½oz) wholewheat
  couscous
175ml (6fl oz) boiling water
Salt

I absolutely love caponata – whether cold on toast, stirred through pasta or, like this, with couscous. This is a slight twist on the authentic dish, just to make life a little easier.

CAPONATA WITH COUSCOUS

In a large, heavy-based frying pan over a medium heat, sauté the onion and garlic in a little olive oil, along with a good pinch of salt, for about 10 minutes until softened.

Add the aubergine and continue to sauté for 10 minutes.

Add the courgette, fresh tomatoes, capers, olives and about half of the chopped tomatoes. Stir thoroughly and bring to a simmer. Cook for 10 minutes until the sauce has reduced and the mix is becoming dry.

Add the rest of the chopped tomatoes, plus the red wine vinegar and dried mixed herbs, then simmer for another 10 minutes until the sauce has reduced again and the flavours have concentrated.

Meanwhile, place the couscous in a bowl, add the boiling water and cover for 10 minutes. Fluff up with a fork.

To serve, divide the couscous between 2 plates and add a portion of the caponata alongside.

This is a zingy, flavoursome vegetable curry with a lovely vibrant colour.

GREEN MASALA WITH PEAS, CARROTS AND COURGETTES

RICH IN:
Beta-carotene
Inulin
Vitamin K

SERVES: 4
150g (5½oz) brown rice
Olive oil, for sautéing
250g (9oz) courgettes,
    cut into half circles
250g (9oz) carrots, sliced
400ml (14fl oz) can
    coconut milk
150g (5½oz) frozen peas
Salt and black pepper

For the curry paste
Handful of coriander leaves
Small handful of mint leaves
4–5 basil leaves
1 green chilli
3 garlic cloves
Thumb-sized piece of fresh
    root ginger, peeled and
    roughly chopped
1 onion, roughly chopped
1 teaspoon garam masala
1 teaspoon ground turmeric

Cook the rice in a large saucepan of boiling water according to the packet instructions.

Meanwhile, place the curry paste ingredients in a food processor and blitz into a smooth paste.

In a heavy-based frying pan over a medium heat, sauté the paste in a little olive oil, along with a good pinch of salt, for about 15–20 minutes until it darkens in colour and is less aggressive on the eyes (you will see exactly what I mean). It's very pungent, so it needs a good cook. Give it a taste and, if it has mellowed, add the courgettes, carrots and coconut milk and simmer for 10 minutes until the veg is cooked. Add the peas and simmer for a final 2–3 minutes.

Season with black pepper and serve with the rice.

SERVES: 2
150g (5½oz) flat rice noodles
1 large red onion, halved
    and sliced
2 large spring onions,
    cut into batons
3 garlic cloves, finely chopped
1 small red chilli, deseeded
    and finely chopped
Olive oil, for sautéing
150g (5½oz) shiitake
    mushrooms, sliced
200g (7oz) firm tofu, cubed
1 tablespoon soy sauce
Juice of 1 lime
1 tablespoon maple syrup
Small coriander sprig,
    roughly chopped,
    to garnish

Simple, tasty and reminiscent of the creations found in your favourite noodle joint.

TOFU SHIITAKE RICE NOODLES

Place the noodles in a saucepan, cover with boiling water and cook according to the packet instructions. Drain and set aside.

Meanwhile, in a large, heavy-based frying pan over a medium heat, sauté the onion, spring onions, garlic and chilli in a little olive oil, along with a good pinch of salt, for about 10 minutes until softened.

Add the sliced shiitake mushrooms and sauté for another 5–6 minutes.

Add the tofu and the noodles and toss together well, then add the soy sauce, lime juice and maple syrup. Toss together well again.

Garnish with the coriander before serving.

4 READY IN A HURRY

Despite our best intentions, sometimes life just gets in the way and we find ourselves pushed for time. These are often the moments when we reach for convenient but less-than-healthy options. This is where these simple, super-speedy, throw-together, nutritious dishes can help.

This is seriously filling, flavoursome, quick and easy. Wraps make a great portable lunch.

SERVES: 1
200g (7oz) canned black
   beans, drained
Juice of ½ lime
½ teaspoon garlic powder
1 wholemeal tortilla wrap
½ ripe avocado, sliced
2 tablespoons canned
   sweetcorn
½ red onion, sliced
Red chilli slices, to taste
Handful of coriander, torn
Salt and black pepper, to taste

MEXICAN WRAP

Place the black beans in a bowl, squeeze over the lime juice and add the garlic powder. Mash with a fork and add a little salt to taste.

Spread the bean mash over the wrap. Top with the avocado, sweetcorn, onion, coriander and chilli slices, then roll it up.

Wrap and keep in the refrigerator if you're making this ahead of time.

I got the idea for this dish from an Indian restaurant near my home. I had never tasted anything quite like it. Since playing around with the recipe, it has morphed from an Indian-style dish into more of a South East Asian one, and I feel it is at its best with this flavour profile. One-pot bliss.

RICH IN:
Calcium
Flavonoids
Vitamin E

SERVES: 4
1 large red onion,
    roughly chopped
3 garlic cloves,
    finely chopped
3 star anise
Olive oil, for sautéing
1 large aubergine, diced
400ml (14fl oz) can
    coconut milk
2 tablespoons crunchy
    peanut butter
1 tablespoon soy sauce
½ teaspoon Chinese
    five-spice
Salt

PEANUT AND COCONUT AUBERGINE

In a large, heavy-based saucepan over a medium heat, sauté the onion, garlic and star anise in a little olive oil, along with a good pinch of salt, for about 10 minutes until softened.

Add the diced aubergine, coconut milk, peanut butter and soy sauce. Mix well and simmer for another 10 minutes until the aubergine is cooked and you get a thick, rich sauce.

Add the five-spice and simmer for another minute before serving.

SERVES: 1
2 large field mushrooms, sliced
Olive oil, for drizzling
1 teaspoon Mexican seasoning
1 large ripe avocado
Juice of ½ lime
1 red chilli, deseeded and
    roughly chopped
1 large garlic clove, crushed
2 corn taco shells
½ red onion, finely chopped
½ ripe mango, diced
Small coriander sprig,
    chopped
Salt

A plant-based twist on a family favourite.
These tacos make a great evening meal.

ROASTED MUSHROOM TACOS

Preheat the oven to 200°C (400°F), Gas Mark 6.

Place the sliced mushrooms in a bowl. Drizzle over a small amount of olive oil and sprinkle with the Mexican seasoning. Toss well.

Spread the mushrooms out on a baking tray and place in the oven for about 20 minutes.

Meanwhile, scoop the avocado flesh into a small bowl. Add the lime juice, chilli, garlic and salt to taste, then mash coarsely.

Divide the avocado mash between the taco shells, then top with the cooked mushrooms, onion, mango and coriander. Serve immediately.

B vitamins
Calcium
Flavonoids
Glucosinolates
Magnesium
Selenium

SERVES: 4
1 red onion, finely sliced
3 garlic cloves, finely chopped
Olive oil, for sautéing
5–6 broccoli florets
5–6 tablespoons water
160g (5¾oz) firm or
    marinated tofu
200g (7oz) pre-cooked brown
    rice (from a sachet)
1 tablespoon soy sauce
2 teaspoons toasted
    sesame oil
2 teaspoons hoisin sauce
Salt

*Stir-fried rice is one of those staple dishes that is
great at the end of a long day when you don't want to
spend ages in the kitchen, but you do want something
nutritious and moreish.*

TOFU, BROCCOLI AND RED ONION FRIED RICE

In a large, heavy-based frying pan over a medium
heat, sauté the onion and garlic in a little olive oil,
along with a good pinch of salt, for about 10 minutes
until softened.

Add the broccoli florets and the measured water and
sauté for around 5–6 minutes, stirring often, until the
broccoli turns a brighter green and starts to soften,
but still retains some bite.

Add the tofu and rice and continue to cook for
3–4 minutes until the rice has softened a little.

Add the soy sauce, sesame oil and hoisin, and cook
for another minute before serving.

The ultimate speedy throw-together that packs plenty of flavour and, of course, a vast nutritional punch. Having cans of pulses to hand in the cupboard is perfect for those days when you want something quick and convenient.

RICH IN:
B vitamins
Calcium
Iron
Lycopene
Magnesium
Oligosaccharides

SERVES: 4
1 large red onion,
   finely chopped
2 garlic cloves,
   finely chopped
Olive oil, for sautéing
400g (14oz) can black-eyed
   beans, drained
300g (10½oz) tomatoes,
   chopped
2 handfuls of baby spinach
½ teaspoon dried mixed herbs
Salt and black pepper
4 slices of sourdough toast,
   to serve (optional)

BLACK-EYED BEAN, TOMATO, RED ONION AND SPINACH SAUTÉ

In a large, heavy-based frying pan over a medium heat, sauté the onion and garlic in a little olive oil, along with a good pinch of salt, for about 10 minutes until softened.

Add the beans and the chopped tomatoes and sauté for 10 minutes, stirring often, until the tomatoes have softened and reduced.

Add the baby spinach and dried herbs, season, and cook for a few minutes until the spinach has wilted.

This is great on its own or served on a slice of sourdough toast.

SERVES: 2
1 large aubergine, diced
½ red onion, finely chopped
2 garlic cloves, finely chopped
Olive oil, for roasting
¼ teaspoon ground cumin
¼ teaspoon ground cinnamon
½ teaspoon smoked paprika
2 slices of multigrain or
   wholemeal bread
Salt
Coriander sprig, chopped,
   to garnish

For the tahini sauce
2 tablespoons tahini
1 tablespoon lemon juice
2–3 tablespoons water

This is a lovely light evening snack that is bursting with flavour. So easy and so tasty.

SPICED AUBERGINE MASH-UP ON TOAST

Preheat the oven to 200°C (400°F), Gas Mark 6.

Place the diced aubergine, onion and garlic in a roasting tin and drizzle with a little olive oil. Roast for 25–30 minutes until softened.

Transfer the contents of the tin to a bowl, add the spices and a good pinch of salt, then mash with a fork.

In a separate bowl, mix together the tahini, lemon juice and water.

Toast the bread. Top each slice with the mashed spiced aubergine, then drizzle over the tahini sauce.

Garnish with the coriander before serving.

This nutritious, super-simple and speedy dish is a great combination of textures and flavours. Serve with noodles or rice, or as a side to another dish.

PEPPER AND TOFU STIR-FRY

SERVES: 4
150g (5½oz) firm tofu, diced
Olive oil, for stir-frying
1 large red onion, sliced
3 garlic cloves, finely chopped
1 large red pepper,
    cored, deseeded and
    sliced lengthways
1 large yellow pepper,
    cored, deseeded and
    sliced lengthways
 1 tablespoon maple syrup
1 tablespoon toasted
    sesame oil
1 tablespoon soy sauce

In a wok or heavy-based frying pan set over a medium heat, fry the tofu in a little olive oil until golden, then transfer to a plate and set aside.

Return the pan to the heat, add a little more olive oil and stir-fry the onion, garlic and peppers, along with a good pinch of salt, until softened.

Return the tofu to the pan. Add the maple syrup, sesame oil and soy sauce, then stir-fry for 3–4 minutes until the sauce thickens. Serve immediately.

This is a simple dish that is full of beautiful, clean flavours – and, of course, nutrients.

RICH IN:
B vitamins
Flavonoids
Inulin

SERVES: 2
1 large leek, sliced
2 garlic cloves,
　finely chopped
Olive oil, for sautéing
1 large fennel bulb,
　thinly sliced
140g (5oz) wholewheat
　linguine
2 teaspoons vegan
　butter alternative
Small dill sprig,
　roughly chopped
Salt and black pepper

LINGUINE WITH SAUTÉED LEEKS AND FENNEL

In a large, heavy-based saucepan over a medium heat, sauté the leek and garlic in a little olive oil, along with a good pinch of salt, for 7–8 minutes until the leeks have softened.

Add the sliced fennel and continue to sauté for another 6–8 minutes.

Meanwhile, add the linguine to a pan of salted boiling water. Cook, according to the packet instructions, until al dente, then drain.

Add the linguine to the saucepan with the leeks and fennel and toss together well. Add the vegan butter and the chopped dill and toss again. Season to taste before serving.

This is one of my all-time favourite salads. There is a lot going on in terms of flavour and texture. The sweetness from the roasted red onions and the figs, the pepperiness of the rocket, the freshness of the radicchio and the punch of the dressing all come together for a real taste explosion.

RICH IN:
Calcium
Flavonoids
Selenium
Vitamin C

SERVES: 2
1 large red onion, sliced
Olive oil, for roasting
1 teaspoon maple syrup
Large handful of rocket leaves
1 radicchio head, chopped
Large handful of baby spinach
2 large figs, cut into wedges

For the dressing
1 tablespoon balsamic vinegar
2 teaspoons maple syrup
1 teaspoon toasted sesame oil
1 tablespoon olive oil

FIG, RADICCHIO AND ROASTED RED ONION SALAD WITH BALSAMIC DRESSING

Preheat the oven to 200°C (400°F), Gas Mark 6.

Place the onion in a roasting tin and drizzle with a little olive oil and the maple syrup. Toss well, then roast for around 20–25 minutes until softened and caramelized.

In a small bowl or jug, whisk together the dressing ingredients.

Plate up the rocket, radicchio and spinach first, then lay the figs on top and dot around the roasted onions.

Pour over the dressing and toss well before serving.

SERVES: 4

1 large red onion, sliced
3 garlic cloves, finely chopped
Olive oil, for sautéing
1–2 tablespoons curry paste
  (madras and balti work well)
400g (14oz) can chopped
  tomatoes
200g (7oz) broad beans
200g (7oz) green beans,
  topped and tailed
3 handfuls of shredded
  spring greens

This is a super-fast curry that makes good use of the green vegetables that are so often seen as bland and boring. Using a shop-bought curry paste saves you time and a lot of faffing around on busy days. Great served with dairy-free yogurt and flatbreads.

CURRIED BEANS AND GREENS

In a heavy-based frying pan over a medium heat, sauté the onion and garlic in a little olive oil, along with a good pinch of salt, for about 10 minutes until softened.

Add the curry paste and sauté for another minute.

Add the chopped tomatoes, broad beans and green beans. Reduce the heat and simmer for 15–20 minutes until the tomatoes have reduced down and a thick curry sauce has formed.

Add the spring greens and cook for a final 3–4 minutes until wilted, then serve.

This is a beautiful, fresh, summery salad that is packed to the hilt with vitamin C. You can find pomegranate molasses in most supermarkets now, or try your local health-food store.

RICH IN:
Beta-carotene
Glucosinolates
Magnesium
Vitamin C

SERVES: 2
2 ripe peaches, halved, stoned
  and cut into wedges
2 handfuls of rocket leaves
3 handfuls of baby spinach
4 tablespoons pomegranate
  seeds

For the dressing
2 teaspoons pomegranate
  molasses
1 teaspoon red wine vinegar
1 tablespoon olive oil
¼ teaspoon garlic salt

GRIDDLED PEACH, ROCKET, SPINACH AND POMEGRANATE SALAD

Place the peach slices on a hot griddle pan over a low heat and gently cook for 4–6 minutes, turning halfway, until they're golden on each side.

Combine the rocket and spinach and divide between 2 plates. Place the griddled peaches on top, then sprinkle over the pomegranate seeds.

In a small bowl or jug, mix together all the dressing ingredients until well combined. Pour over each salad and serve.

5 MINIMAL EFFORT

This chapter is all about convenience – meals that can be thrown together at a moment's notice. These are the types of dishes that are perfect prepared on the hop, or that you can whip up the night before and throw into a lunch box for the next day!

RICH IN:
B vitamins
Calcium
Selenium
Vitamin E

SERVES: 4
2 teaspoons soy sauce
1 tablespoon maple syrup
½ teaspoon mild curry powder
200g (7oz) firm tofu, cubed
150g (5½oz) brown rice

For the satay dipping sauce
2 heaped tablespoons
  crunchy peanut butter
2 heaped teaspoons vegan
  Thai red curry paste
4 tablespoons coconut milk
1 garlic clove, crushed

To serve
Lime wedges
Red chilli slices

I have been lucky enough to spend a lot of time out in Malaysia, and one of my favourite street-food dishes there is satay. It's utterly addictive. It takes a little time to marinate the tofu, but it's well worth it. Serve with some stir-fried greens or brown rice.

BAKED TOFU SATAY

Preheat the oven to 200°C (400°F), Gas Mark 6. Line a baking tray with tin foil.

In a bowl, mix together the soy sauce, maple syrup and curry powder. Add the tofu and marinate for 1–2 hours.

Thread the tofu cubes on to skewers, about 4–5 cubes per skewer. Place the tofu skewers on the prepared baking tray and bake in the oven for around 25 minutes, turning once halfway through the cooking time.

Meanwhile, cook the rice in a large pan of boiling water according to the packet instructions, then drain.

Place all the dipping sauce ingredients in a small saucepan and mix together until smooth, adding a little more coconut milk if needed. Heat gently over a low heat until thickened.

Serve the tofu skewers with the rice and the satay sauce for dipping, garnished with red chilli slices and accompanied by lime wedges for squeezing over.

I really do love a throw-everything-together traybake. All you need is one large roasting tin and your dinner plates. They require little preparation, and, best of all, the washing-up is kept to a minimum. Rich, concentrated flavours can develop because the ingredients are slowly roasted all together.

RICH IN:
Beta-carotene
Flavonoids
Inulin

SERVES: 4
½ large unpeeled butternut squash, cut into large dice
1 large red onion, sliced
4 garlic cloves, roughly chopped
Olive oil, for drizzling
400g (14oz) mixed tomatoes, halved, or quartered if large
1 teaspoon ground cinnamon
1 teaspoon ground cumin
120g (4½oz) wholewheat couscous
1 teaspoon vegetable stock powder
175ml (6fl oz) boiling water
Salt

SPICED SQUASH TRAYBAKE WITH COUSCOUS

Preheat the oven to 200°C (400°F), Gas Mark 6.

Place the squash, red onion and garlic in a roasting tin, drizzle with a small amount of olive oil and add a good pinch of salt. Place in the oven to roast for 20 minutes.

Add the tomatoes, cinnamon and cumin, and stir everything together well. Roast in the oven for another 20–25 minutes, or until the squash has softened and concentrated juices have formed from the tomatoes.

Meanwhile, place the couscous in a bowl along with the stock powder. Add the boiling water and cover for 10 minutes, then fluff up with a fork. If still slightly al dente, add a bit more boiling water and let it sit for a few more minutes.

Serve the roasted vegetables with the couscous.

SERVES: 4

1 large red onion,
   finely chopped
3 garlic cloves,
   finely chopped
Thumb-sized piece of
   fresh root ginger, peeled
   and finely chopped
Olive oil, for sautéing
2 tablespoons balti
   curry paste
1 large cauliflower,
   broken into small florets
400g (14oz) can chopped
   tomatoes
400ml (14fl oz) can
   coconut milk
160g (5¾oz) fresh or
   frozen peas
Salt and black pepper
150g (5½oz) brown rice,
   to serve

This is a great option for those days when you want to throw something together fast. There are other curry recipes in this book where we make the paste from scratch, and that's great. But at the end of a long day, do you want to do that? A good curry paste will save your skin when you're short on time.

EASY CAULIFLOWER AND PEA CURRY

In a large, heavy-based saucepan over a medium heat, sauté the onion, garlic and ginger in a little olive oil, along with a good pinch of salt, for about 10 minutes until softened.

Add the curry paste, cauliflower florets, chopped tomatoes and coconut milk. Season, and then reduce the heat and simmer for 25–30 minutes, adding the peas for the final 5 minutes, until the sauce has reduced and intensified in flavour and the cauliflower is cooked through.

Meanwhile, cook the rice in a large pan of boiling water according to the packet instructions. Drain, then serve with the curry.

SERVES: 6
1 large red onion,
  finely chopped
2 garlic cloves,
  finely chopped
1 small red chilli, deseeded
  and finely chopped
Olive oil, for sautéing
1kg (2lb 4oz) large
  tomatoes, quartered
3 sun-dried tomatoes
150ml (5fl oz) vegetable stock
500g (1lb 2oz) wholewheat
  penne
2 handfuls of spinach
1 tablespoon tomato purée
Salt and black pepper

So simple, yet so delicious. This is family comfort food at its best. The tomato and chilli sauce is not only great stirred into pasta, it can also be a very good base for lasagne and pizza. The best sun-dried tomatoes to use here are the dry variety, not the ones in oil.

PASTA WITH TOMATO AND CHILLI SAUCE

In a large, heavy-based saucepan over a medium heat, sauté the onion, garlic and chilli in a little olive oil, along with a good pinch of salt, for about 10 minutes until softened.

Add the fresh tomatoes and the sun-dried tomatoes and sauté for 5 minutes. Add the vegetable stock, reduce the heat and simmer for about 20–30 minutes until the tomatoes have broken down and a rich sauce has formed.

Meanwhile, add the penne to a pan of salted boiling water. Cook, according to the packet instructions, until al dente. Drain and set aside.

Add the spinach to the sauce and stir through for a couple of minutes until wilted. Stir in the tomato purée, then transfer the sauce to a food processor or blender and blitz until smooth. Season to taste.

Stir the sauce through the cooked penne and serve.

SERVES: 4
1 large beetroot, diced
1 celeriac, diced
Olive oil, for drizzling
400g (14oz) can chickpeas,
   drained
2–3 rosemary sprigs
50ml (2fl oz) vegetable stock
Salt and black pepper

This is great served with some steamed greens
and a slice of multigrain bread.

BEETROOT, CELERIAC AND CHICKPEA ROAST

Preheat the oven to 200°C (400°F), Gas Mark 6.

Place the beetroot and celeriac in a roasting tin, drizzle with a little olive oil, season with salt and black pepper and roast for 10 minutes.

Remove from the oven and add the chickpeas and rosemary. Toss together well and roast for another 20 minutes.

Remove from the oven again and add the vegetable stock, then return to the oven and roast for another 30 minutes.

Serve immediately.

Beta-carotene
Calcium
Lignans
Selenium
Soluble fibre
Zinc

SERVES: 2

2 sweet potatoes
2 tablespoons tahini
½ red onion, finely chopped
4–5 pitted green olives,
    roughly chopped
200g (7oz) canned cannellini
    beans, drained
Small sprig of coriander,
    roughly chopped
Salt
Mixed salad, to serve

These are bursting with flavour. You can load them up with pretty much anything that's kicking around in the fridge.

TWICE-BAKED SWEET POTATO BOATS

Preheat oven to 200°C (400°F), Gas Mark 6.

Prick the sweet potatoes all over, place on a baking tray and bake for around 45 minutes until soft. Scoop out the flesh into a bowl and place the skins (boats) back on the baking tray.

Add the tahini, red onion, olives, cannellini beans and coriander to the bowl, along with a good pinch of salt. Mix together well.

Spoon the mixture into the empty sweet potato skins and place them back in the oven to bake for 20 minutes.

Serve with a hearty side salad.

RICH IN:
Beta-carotene
Lycopene
Vitamin C

SERVES: 2
1 large red onion, sliced
1 large red pepper, cored,
   deseeded and sliced
1 large yellow pepper, cored,
   deseeded and sliced
4 large garlic cloves,
   finely chopped
Olive oil, for drizzling
4–5 large plum tomatoes,
   quartered
1 tablespoon balsamic vinegar
100g (3½oz) orzo
200–300ml (7–10fl oz)
   vegetable stock
Salt
Small basil sprig, leaves
   picked, to garnish

This is real comfort food and a great one for those busier evenings when you don't have time to be faffing around. Simple, yet flavoursome. What's better than that?

ORZO WITH ROASTED VEGETABLE SAUCE

Preheat the oven to 200°C (400°F), Gas Mark 6.

Place the onion, peppers and garlic in a roasting tin, drizzle with a little olive oil and add a good pinch of salt. Roast for about 20 minutes. Add the tomatoes and balsamic vinegar and stir. Return to the oven and roast for a further 25–30 minutes.

At this stage, there should be a lovely concentrated sauce in the bottom of the roasting tin. Transfer everything to a food processor and blitz.

Pour the sauce into a saucepan, add the orzo and simmer gently for about 10 minutes until the sauce has thickened and reduced and the orzo is starting to soften. Add the vegetable stock in small increments. You probably won't need all of it. What you are aiming for is a risotto-like texture, where the orzo is cooked al dente and the sauce is thick and rich.

Garnish with basil leaves before serving.

This dish has a beautiful, lingering, rich flavour. It works as a light meal in its own right or served with a green vegetable like broccoli.

RICH IN:
Carotenoids
Flavonoids

SWEET POTATO, RED ONION AND CHERRY TOMATO TRAYBAKE

SERVES: 4
1 large sweet potato,
   skin on, diced
1 large red onion, thinly sliced
15–24 cherry tomatoes, on the
   vine (depending on how
   big the tomatoes are)
3 garlic cloves, finely chopped
Olive oil, for drizzling
125ml (4fl oz) vegan white wine
Salt and black pepper, to taste

Preheat the oven to 200°C (400°F), Gas Mark 6.

Place the sweet potato, onion, tomatoes (still on the vine) and garlic in a roasting tin. Drizzle with olive oil and add a pinch of salt and black pepper. Roast for 10 minutes.

Remove from the oven and add the white wine. Roast for another 40 minutes until a thick sauce has formed.

This interesting dish is packed full of flavour. Roasted broccoli is just incredible. Once tried, always loved.

SERVES: 4
500g (1lb 2oz) new
   potatoes, halved
1 broccoli, broken
   into florets
Olive oil, for roasting
1 teaspoon maple syrup
2 teaspoons mild
   curry powder
½ teaspoon garlic salt

CURRIED NEW POTATO AND BROCCOLI ROAST

Preheat the oven to 200°C (400°F), Gas Mark 6.

Place the potatoes and broccoli in a roasting tin and drizzle with olive oil and the maple syrup. Toss well, then add the curry powder and garlic salt and toss well again to ensure the potatoes and broccoli are coated.

Roast for 35–40 minutes until the potatoes and broccoli are cooked through and crispy at the edges.

Serve immediately.

6 TIME ON YOUR HANDS

Sometimes we just want to get into the kitchen and create a masterpiece; something that is a little more special, but probably takes a little more effort. Maybe there are a few extra steps, some fiddly processes, or perhaps the cooking time is just longer.

While I often create recipes that fit into our busy modern lives, I do believe that food is a celebration of the senses. A variety of textures, flavours and colours should come together to create an indulgent and decadent experience from time to time, too.

RICH IN:
Calcium
Flavonoids
Lycopene
Selenium
Vitamin E
Zinc

SERVES: 4
2 large aubergines,
    sliced lengthways
    into 5mm (¼in) slices
Olive oil, for sautéing
1 large red onion,
    finely chopped
3 garlic cloves,
    finely chopped
400g (14oz) can green
    lentils, drained
200g (7oz) tomato passata
½ teaspoon ground cumin
1 teaspoon ground cinnamon
Salt
Mustard cress, to garnish
    (optional)

For the tahini sauce
2 tablespoons tahini
4 tablespoons lemon juice
1 large garlic clove
4–5 tablespoons hot water

This divine dish has a Middle Eastern vibe and is absolutely bursting with flavour – and it's incredibly nutrient-dense.

LENTIL-STUFFED AUBERGINE ROLLS WITH TAHINI SAUCE

In a large, heavy-based frying pan over a medium heat, lightly fry the aubergine slices in olive oil for about 5 minutes on each side until softened. Remove from the pan on to some paper towels, pat dry, then set aside and keep warm.

In the same pan, sauté the onion and garlic in a little olive oil, along with a good pinch of salt, for about 10 minutes until softened.

Add the lentils, passata and spices, along with another good pinch of salt, then simmer for 20–25 minutes until it has reduced to a thick ragout-like sauce.

Meanwhile, to make the tahini sauce, place the tahini, lemon juice, garlic and hot water in a food processor and blend. If the sauce is too thick, add more hot water bit by bit, until a thin, spreadable sauce has formed.

To serve, take 4 plates and smear a generous dollop of tahini sauce across each one. Add a couple of teaspoons of the lentil mixture to the centre of an aubergine slice, roll it up, then place on top of the tahini sauce. Repeat until all the aubergine slices and lentils have been used up. Garnish with mustard cress, if using.

A very fancy-looking dish, and a great one to bring out at a dinner party.

RICH IN:
Beta-carotene
B vitamins
Oligosaccharides
Zinc

SERVES: 2
300g (10½oz) baby carrots, tops removed
Olive oil, for roasting
1 teaspoon toasted sesame oil
1 teaspoon maple syrup
¼ teaspoon garlic salt
2 tablespoons hazelnuts, roughly crushed
2 handfuls of micro salad
1 tablespoon lemon juice
Salt and black pepper

For the butter bean purée
400g (14oz) can butter beans, drained
1 large garlic clove, finely chopped
¼ teaspoon ground turmeric
4-5 tablespoons water

ROASTED BABY CARROTS ON TURMERIC BUTTER BEAN PURÉE

Preheat the oven to 200°C (400°F), Gas Mark 6.

Place the carrots in a roasting tin. Add a drizzle of olive oil, along with the sesame oil, maple syrup and garlic salt, then roast for 20–25 minutes until softened.

Meanwhile, make the butter bean purée. Place the butter beans, garlic, turmeric and measured water in a blender, and blitz until you have a smooth consistency.

In a dry frying pan over a low heat, toast the hazelnuts, along with a pinch of salt, for about 2 minutes until golden brown. Remove from the pan and lightly crush.

In a bowl, dress the micro salad with the lemon juice and some black pepper.

Take 2 plates and place a dollop of butter bean purée in the centre of each one. Top each with half the roasted carrots, sprinkle over the toasted hazelnuts, then finish with the micro salad and serve.

A barlotto is a risotto made with pearl barley instead of rice. This delicious grain does take longer to cook, but the nutritional punch it packs is so worth it.

RICH IN:
Beta-carotene
B vitamins
Flavonoids
Inulin
Magnesium

SERVES: 4
1 large sweet potato,
    skin on, diced
1 large red onion, sliced
Olive oil, for drizzling
    and sautéing
1 large white onion,
    finely chopped
3 garlic cloves,
    finely chopped
250g (9oz) pearl barley
1 litre (1¾ pints) vegetable
    stock (you may not need
    all of this)
175ml (6fl oz) vegan
    white wine
2 large handfuls of
    baby spinach
Salt and black pepper

RED ONION, SWEET POTATO AND SPINACH BARLOTTO

Preheat the oven to 200°C (400°F), Gas Mark 6.

Place the diced sweet potato and sliced red onion in a roasting tin. Drizzle with a little olive oil, season with salt and black pepper, then roast for 25–30 minutes.

In a large, heavy-based saucepan over a medium heat, sauté the white onion and garlic in a little olive oil, along with a good pinch of salt, for about 10 minutes until softened.

Add the pearl barley and start adding the vegetable stock, bit by bit, stirring often. When the stock has been absorbed, add a little more, and so on, until the pearl barley is cooked and has a creamy, risotto-like texture. This will take about 25 minutes in total. Add the white wine and simmer for another 3–5 minutes.

Finally, stir in the baby spinach and allow it to wilt.

Spoon a generous helping of the barlotto in the centre of each plate, then top with the roasted sweet potato and red onion mixture. Garnish with black pepper and serve immediately.

RICH IN:
Betacyanin
Calcium
Inulin
Magnesium
Vitamin C

SERVES: 2
2 large beetroots,
    cut into wedges
2 large white onions,
    finely chopped
1 garlic clove,
    finely chopped
1 tablespoon olive oil,
    plus extra for drizzling
    and sautéing
2 heaped teaspoons hot
    horseradish sauce
1–3 tablespoons water
Large handful of watercress
Large handful of rocket
Small mint sprig,
    roughly chopped
1 large orange, peeled
    and thinly sliced
4 tablespoons lemon juice
Salt and black pepper

ROASTED BEETROOT ON WHITE ONION AND HORSERADISH PURÉE

Preheat the oven to 200°C (400°F), Gas Mark 6.

Place the beetroot wedges in a roasting tin. Drizzle with olive oil, sprinkle with a pinch of salt, then roast for 30–40 minutes.

Meanwhile, in a small saucepan over a medium heat, sauté the onions and garlic in a little olive oil, along with a good pinch of salt, for about 10 minutes until the onion has softened. Add the horseradish sauce, then blitz into a purée using a stick blender (or transfer to a blender or food processor). Add the measured water in small increments until the purée reaches the desired thick consistency.

In a bowl, combine the watercress, rocket, mint and orange slices. Squeeze over the lemon juice and drizzle over the olive oil, then toss everything together.

Serve the roasted beetroots on top of the purée with the salad on the side. Garnish with black pepper.

This is an unusual dish with flavours ranging from earthy to tangy to aromatic. They may seem a little odd, but when they're combined, they definitely work!

RICH IN:
Calcium
Flavonoids
Lutein
Magnesium
Potassium
Vitamin C
Vitamin K

SERVES: 4
6 large cavolo nero leaves,
    tough stalks removed
Olive oil, for drizzling
1 large fennel bulb, sliced
260g (9½oz) canned
    sweetcorn, drained
1½ tablespoons vegan
    soft cheese
¼ teaspoon garlic salt
Salt and black pepper

For the pickled red onions
1 large red onion,
    thinly sliced
1 teaspoon fennel seeds
300ml (10fl oz) red
    wine vinegar

ROASTED FENNEL, 'CREAMED' CORN, CRISPY CAVOLO NERO AND PICKLED RED ONIONS

Make the pickled red onions the night before. Place the sliced onions in a bowl with the fennel seeds, cover with the red wine vinegar, then leave in the fridge overnight.

When you're ready to cook, preheat the oven to 180°C (350°F), Gas Mark 4.

To make the crispy cavolo nero, roughly tear the leaves into a bowl. Add a small drizzle of olive oil and a pinch of salt, gently toss, then spread out on a baking tray and place in the oven for around 10 minutes until crispy. Remove from the oven and set aside to cool.

Place the fennel in a roasting tin, drizzle with olive oil and add a good pinch each of salt and black pepper. Increase the oven temperature to 200°C (400°F), Gas Mark 6, and roast the fennel for 25 minutes, or until cooked through and golden.

Meanwhile, in a saucepan over a medium heat, combine the sweetcorn, vegan cheese and garlic salt, along with a pinch of pepper, then cook, stirring occasionally, for 5 minutes until warmed through.

To serve, place a portion of the 'creamed' corn on each plate. Top with crispy cavolo nero, then the roasted fennel slices, and finish with the pickled red onions.

This has a real summer vibe, with so many textures and layers of flavour. It makes the perfect dinner on a warm evening.

BALSAMIC PEPPER AND RED ONION TRAYBAKE WITH LENTIL SALAD AND CARROT-GINGER PURÉE

RICH IN:
Beta-carotene
Flavonoids
Soluble fibre

SERVES: 4
2 large peppers, cored,
    deseeded and quartered
1 large red onion,
    cut into 8 wedges
Olive oil, for roasting
½ teaspoon garlic powder
1 tablespoon balsamic vinegar
1 teaspoon maple syrup
Salt

For the carrot-ginger purée
½ red onion, finely chopped
2 garlic cloves, finely chopped
thumb-sized piece of fresh root
    ginger, peeled and chopped
4 large carrots, diced
2 teaspoons vegetable
    stock powder

For the lentil salad
400g (14oz) can Puy
    lentils, drained
Large bunch of curly leaf
    parsley, finely chopped
1 teaspoon capers, chopped

Preheat the oven to 200°C (400°F), Gas Mark 6.

Place the peppers and onion in a roasting tin, drizzle with a little olive oil, add a good pinch of salt and roast for 15 minutes. Add the garlic powder, balsamic vinegar and maple syrup, give everything a good stir, then return to the oven for another 20 minutes.

Meanwhile, make the purée. In a heavy-based saucepan over a medium heat, sauté the onion, garlic and ginger in a little olive oil, along with a good pinch of salt, for about 10 minutes until softened. Add the diced carrots, the stock powder and enough water to almost cover everything, then simmer for 10 minutes until the carrots have softened. At this point, blitz into a smooth purée using a stick blender (or transfer to a blender or food processor).

Make the lentil salad by mixing together the lentils, parsley and capers.

To plate up, spoon a portion of the purée in the centre of each plate. Pile on the lentil salad, then top with a helping of the traybake.

SERVES: 2
2 large flat mushrooms or
  4 smaller flat mushrooms
Handful of flat-leaf parsley
  leaves, to garnish (optional)

For the nut filling
5 button mushrooms
5–6 sun-dried tomatoes in oil
5 tablespoons mixed nuts
  (walnuts, almonds and
  hazelnuts all work well)
1 large red onion, chopped
2 garlic cloves, finely chopped
2 tablespoons breadcrumbs
1 teaspoon dried mixed herbs
1 tablespoon olive oil

For the cassoulet
1 large red onion, chopped
3 garlic cloves, finely chopped
Olive oil, for sautéing
2 × 400g (14oz) cans cannellini
  beans, drained, a third of
  the liquid retained
2 teaspoons vegetable
  stock powder
Salt and black pepper

*This delivers a multitude of flavours and textures.
It's great on its own or served as an accompaniment
to a Sunday roast.*

STUFFED FIELD MUSHROOMS ON WHITE BEAN CASSOULET

Preheat the oven to 200°C (400°F), Gas Mark 6.

Place all the ingredients for the nut filling, apart
from the breadcrumbs, dried herbs and oil, into
a food processor and blitz into a doughy paste.

Remove as much of the thick central stalk from the
flat mushrooms as possible, then place on a baking
tray with the stem side facing upwards. Scoop the
nut mixture into the mushrooms.

In a bowl, mix together the breadcrumbs, dried herbs
and oil, then spoon on top of the nut mixture.

Place the mushrooms in the oven for 25–30 minutes.

While the mushrooms are cooking, make the cassoulet.
In a heavy-based saucepan over a medium heat, sauté
the onion and garlic in a little olive oil, along with a
good pinch of salt, for about 10 minutes until softened.

Add the beans and their reserved liquid, along with the
stock powder, then simmer for 10–15 minutes, stirring
occasionally, until you have a creamy bean stew.

Dollop a helping of the cassoulet in the centre of
each plate, then place the stuffed mushrooms on
top. Garnish with parsley leaves, if using, and serve.

SERVES: 2
2 large potatoes
Mixed salad, to serve

For the ratatouille
1 large red onion,
    finely chopped
3 garlic cloves,
    finely chopped
Olive oil, for sautéing
1 large red pepper, cored,
    deseeded and cut into
    2cm (1in) chunks
1 large courgette,
    cut into half rounds
½ aubergine, diced
400g (14oz) tomato passata
Salt

A comforting yet easy dinner that is perfect for a cold evening. You could forgo the potatoes and serve the ratatouille with brown rice or quinoa, or even stir through pasta.

RATATOUILLE-TOPPED BAKED POTATO

Preheat the oven to 200°C (400°F), Gas Mark 6.

Place the potatoes on a baking tray and place in the oven for 1 hour, or until the potatoes are crispy on the outside and soft and fluffy on the inside.

Meanwhile, make the ratatouille in a heavy-based frying pan over a medium heat, sauté the onion and garlic in a little olive oil, along with a good pinch of salt, for 2–3 minutes.

Add the rest of the vegetables and continue to sauté for 7–8 minutes until they have softened.

Add the passata and simmer for around 20 minutes until all the vegetables are cooked and the sauce has reduced.

Halve the baked potatoes, scoop out the flesh and transfer it to a mixing bowl. Add the ratatouille to the bowl and mix together before spooning back into the potato skins. Return to the oven for 15 minutes.

Serve with a large side salad.

RICH IN:
Calcium
Flavonoids
Lignans
Magnesium
Selenium
Vitamin K
Zinc

SERVES: 2
1 large aubergine,
    halved, flesh scooped
    out, diced and set aside
1 large red onion,
    finely chopped
2 garlic cloves,
    finely chopped
Olive oil, for sautéing
200g (7oz) canned
    chickpeas, drained
200g (7oz) tomato passata
1 teaspoon mild curry powder
4 handfuls of curly kale
Salt

For the tahini sauce
2 tablespoons tahini
4 tablespoons lemon juice
1 garlic clove, finely chopped
4–5 tablespoons hot water

This is a real flavour bomb of a dish. Bursting with Middle Eastern flavours as well as nutrients, this just may turn out to be a regular favourite.

BAKED AUBERGINE AND WILTED KALE WITH TAHINI SAUCE

Preheat the oven to 200°C (400°F), Gas Mark 6.

Place the hollowed-out aubergine halves on a baking tray, skin-side up, and cook for 15 minutes.

Meanwhile, in a heavy-based saucepan over a medium heat, sauté the onion and garlic in a little olive oil, along with a good pinch of salt, for about 10 minutes until softened.

Add the diced aubergine flesh, chickpeas, passata and curry powder, then reduce the heat and simmer for 30 minutes, stirring often, until the mixture has reduced right down.

Remove the aubergine halves from the oven and turn them over. Fill them with the chickpea mixture, pressing down well so it's compact. Place in the oven for another 20 minutes.

Meanwhile, make the tahini sauce by mixing the remaining chopped garlic, tahini and lemon juice together in a bowl. Add the measured water, bit by bit, until the sauce is thin enough to drizzle.

Gently steam the kale in a steamer or in a saucepan with a splash of water for a few minutes until it has wilted.

To serve, divide the kale between 2 plates, then drizzle over half the tahini sauce. Place a stuffed aubergine half on top and finish with the rest of the tahini sauce.

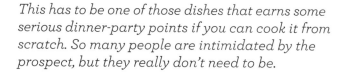

SERVES: 4
Coconut oil, for frying
1 large courgette, sliced
½ red pepper, cored, deseeded
and chopped into chunks
¼ aubergine, sliced
6–7 baby corns, halved
lengthways
100g (3½oz) shiitake
mushrooms, sliced
400ml (14fl oz) coconut milk
200ml (7fl oz) vegetable stock
150g (5½oz) brown rice
2 handfuls of baby spinach

For the green curry paste
2 lemon grass stalks, chopped
2 green chillies
2 garlic cloves
1 large white onion, chopped
1.5cm (½in) piece of fresh root
ginger or galangal, peeled
and chopped
Handful of coriander leaves
4 basil leaves
4 kaffir lime leaves
½ teaspoon ground
white pepper
½ teaspoon ground coriander
3 tablespoons dark soy sauce
1 teaspoon salt
Juice of 1 lime

This has to be one of those dishes that earns some serious dinner-party points if you can cook it from scratch. So many people are intimidated by the prospect, but they really don't need to be.

CLASSIC GREEN CURRY

Place all the paste ingredients in a food processor and blitz to form a pungent, aromatic paste.

In a large, heavy-based saucepan over a medium heat, fry the paste in a little coconut oil for about 5 minutes until it turns a darker shade of green.

Add the courgette, red pepper, aubergine, baby corn, mushrooms, coconut milk and vegetable stock. Simmer for about 15 minutes until the vegetables are cooked.

Meanwhile, cook the rice in a large pan of boiling water according to the packet instructions, then drain.

Finally, add the spinach to the curry and stir through until wilted. Serve with the rice.

SERVES: 4
1 large red onion,
 finely chopped
3 garlic cloves,
 finely chopped
Olive oil, for sautéing
1 large courgette, diced
400g (14oz) can green lentils
 or Puy lentils, drained
400g (14oz) tomato passata
2 teaspoons dried mixed
 herbs (optional)
2 aubergines, sliced
 lengthways into 5mm
 (¼in) slices
100g (3½oz) vegan cheese,
 torn or crumbled
Salt
Rocket salad, to serve

This is a lower-carbohydrate version of the old classic. I have left out a white sauce here, as many of the recipes for a vegan white sauce are pretty fiddly. By all means, if you find one, feel free to top this dish with it. I have also left the option of a vegan cheese open. In an ideal world, a good-quality nut-based cheese would be perfect, but if this is hard to find, use whatever you can get in your local supermarket or health-food store.

AUBERGINE AND LENTIL LASAGNE

Preheat the oven to 200°C (400°F), Gas Mark 6.

In a large, heavy-based saucepan over a medium heat, sauté the onion and garlic in a little olive oil, along with a good pinch of salt, for about 10 minutes until softened.

Add the courgette and continue to sauté for another 4–5 minutes until it begins to soften.

Add the lentils, passata and mixed herbs, if using, reduce the heat and simmer for around 20 minutes until the mixture has reduced down. What you are aiming for is a thick, rich ragù sauce, similar to what you'd find in a traditional lasagne.

Meanwhile, in a large frying pan, gently fry the aubergine slices in a small amount of olive oil for 5 minutes on each side until they have softened.

Spoon a layer of the lentil ragout into the bottom of an ovenproof dish. Cover with some of the aubergine slices. Repeat the layers until the lentils and the aubergine slices are used up. Top with the vegan cheese, then bake for 20–25 minutes until golden brown at the edges and the cheese is bubbling.

Serve immediately with rocket salad.

Beta-carotene
B vitamins
Calcium
Iron
Soluble fibre
Zinc

SERVES: 4
2 large sweet potatoes,
    peeled and diced
1 large red onion,
    finely chopped
3 garlic cloves,
    finely chopped
Olive oil, for sautéing
400g (14oz) can
    chickpeas, drained
150g (5½oz) dried red lentils
400g (14oz) tomato passata
½ teaspoon dried mixed herbs
1 teaspoon vegetable
    stock powder
2 handfuls of baby spinach
Salt and black pepper

This is a regular staple in my household and always goes down a treat. It is real comfort food at its best.

LENTIL AND CHICKPEA SHEPHERD'S PIE

Cook the sweet potatoes in a pan of salted boiling water for about 20 minutes, or until softened. Drain and then mash. Set aside until needed.

Meanwhile, in a saucepan over a medium heat, sauté the onion and garlic in a little olive oil, along with good pinch of salt, until softened.

Add the chickpeas, lentils, passata and dried herbs. Reduce the heat and simmer for 40 minutes, or until the lentils have broken down and the sauce has thickened. You may need to add a little water if it dries out too much, but a thick, rich ragout-like sauce is what you want to end up with. Add the vegetable stock powder and the baby spinach, stirring it through the lentils until it wilts.

Preheat the oven to 200°C (400°F), Gas Mark 6.

Spoon the chickpea ragout into an ovenproof dish. Top with the sweet potato mash, then spread it out evenly and score with a fork. Grind over some black pepper.

Bake the shepherd's pie in the oven for 30 minutes until golden and bubbling.

Serve immediately.

SERVES: 2
350g (12oz) new
    potatoes, halved
Olive oil, for drizzling
    and sautéing
⅔ teaspoon garlic salt
2 teaspoons maple syrup
4 teaspoons water
½ large cauliflower, sliced
    lengthways into 2 steaks
    2cm (1in) thick
½ teaspoon ground cumin
1 teaspoon ground cinnamon
¼ teaspoon smoked
    sweet paprika
1 garlic clove, finely chopped
200g (7oz) frozen peas
200–300ml (7–10fl oz)
    vegetable stock
Salt and black pepper,
    to taste
Handful of micro salad,
    to garnish

The ingredients and flavours in this dish combine beautifully. Cauliflower steaks are so versatile and work well with a whole array of different spices and flavours – so get experimenting! This makes an amazing Sunday lunch alternative.

MOROCCAN-SPICED CAULIFLOWER STEAKS

Preheat the oven to 200°C (400°F), Gas Mark 6.

Parboil the new potatoes in a pan of salted boiling water for about 5 minutes, or until they just begin to soften, then drain. 'Fluff' them up by giving them a good shake in the colander, then tip into a roasting tin. Drizzle over a small amount of olive oil and toss well. Sprinkle over the garlic salt and toss well again. Roast in the oven for 45 minutes until golden and crispy.

Meanwhile, mix together the maple syrup and water, then brush both sides of each cauliflower steak with a thin layer of the mixture. Sprinkle over the cumin, cinnamon and paprika, ensuring both sides are coated. Place the steaks on a baking tray and roast in the oven for around 20–25 minutes until cooked and the edges are turning golden.

Meanwhile, make the purée. In a saucepan over a medium heat, sauté the garlic in olive oil, with a pinch of salt, for a few minutes. Add the peas and enough vegetable stock to half-cover the peas, and simmer for 10 minutes. Transfer everything to a blender (or use a stick blender) and blitz until smooth.

Divide the pea purée between 2 plates, season, then place the cauliflower steaks on top and scatter round the roasted potatoes. Garnish with micro salad, if using.

The absolute classic that is a miso aubergine is a thing of beauty. This flavoursome treat is always one of my go-tos when eating out. Once tried, never forgotten.

RICH IN:
Beta-carotene
Calcium
Flavonoids
Magnesium

MISO AUBERGINE ON CHILLI-GINGER CARROT MASH WITH GARLIC PAK CHOI

SERVES: 2

1 tablespoon brown miso paste
1 tablespoon maple syrup
2 teaspoons toasted sesame oil
2 teaspoons rice wine vinegar
1 large aubergine, halved and flesh deeply scored into diamonds, (avoid cutting the skin)
4 large carrots, chopped
1 small green chilli, deseeded and finely chopped
5mm (¼in) piece of fresh root ginger, peeled and finely chopped or grated
2 garlic cloves, finely chopped
Olive oil, for sautéing
2 pak choi, leaves separated
Salt and black pepper

Mix together the miso, maple syrup, sesame oil and rice wine vinegar. Place the aubergine halves on a baking tray and pour over most of the marinade, filling the cuts and allowing some to flow over. Reserve a small amount of the marinade. Leave to marinate for 30 minutes.

Preheat the oven to 200°C (400°F), Gas Mark 6.

Place the aubergines in the oven for 35–40 minutes. Check every 10–12 minutes to stop them from burning.

Meanwhile, place the carrots in a steamer and steam for 10 minutes until soft enough to crush. Alternatively, put them in a saucepan over a medium heat and cover with water. Place a lid on the pan and simmer for 10 minutes until softened, then drain.

Transfer the cooked carrots to a saucepan, if necessary, and add the chilli and ginger. Mash with a fork and season with salt and black pepper.

In another saucepan over a medium heat, sauté the garlic in olive oil, along with a small pinch of salt. Add the pak choi and sauté for a few minutes until wilted.

Divide the carrot mash between 2 plates and arrange the pak choi alongside. Place an aubergine half on top of the mash and drizzle over the reserved marinade.

7 A BIT ON THE SIDE

Nutritious side dishes help you to find more ways to pile healthy, nutrient-dense ingredients on to your plate. Remember, the more variety the better, and these options will really help you to mix things up.

RICH IN:
Calcium
Glucosinolates
Lignans
Selenium
Vitamin C

SERVES: 4
1 large broccoli, broken
    into florets, then halved
Olive oil, for roasting
½ teaspoon garlic salt
1½ teaspoons smoked sweet
    paprika, plus extra to garnish
½ teaspoon dried mixed herbs

For the tahini drizzle
2½ tablespoons tahini
1 large garlic clove,
    finely chopped
4 tablespoons lemon juice
3–4 tablespoons water
Salt (optional)

If you have never tried roasted broccoli before, get ready to have your mind blown. It's utterly delicious. Even the greatest broccoli haters can be converted with this one!

ROASTED BROCCOLI WITH TAHINI DRIZZLE

Preheat the oven to 200°C (400°F), Gas Mark 6.

Place the broccoli in a roasting tin and drizzle with olive oil. Sprinkle over the garlic salt, paprika and dried herbs. Toss together well.

Place in the oven to roast for around 25–30 minutes. Check on it every 15 minutes or so, and stir if needed to prevent any charring.

Meanwhile, make the tahini drizzle by mixing the tahini, garlic and lemon juice together in a bowl. Add the water, bit by bit, until the sauce is thin enough to drizzle. Season with a little salt, if needed.

Cover the broccoli with the tahini drizzle before serving, garnished with extra paprika.

This is a delicious mayonnaise alternative that is great in a sandwich, or as a dip for chips and wedges.

AVOCADO 'MAYO'

SERVES: 4
1 large, very ripe avocado
3 tablespoons extra virgin
 olive oil
2 tablespoons water
4 tablespoons lemon juice
Salt

Scoop the flesh out of the avocado into a food processor. Add the remaining ingredients, along with a pinch of salt, then blitz until smooth.

This beautiful side dish lends itself well to most types of cuisine. It is as at home with Asian-fusion dishes as it is with Mediterranean flavours. If you have never roasted Brussels sprouts before, you are in for a serious treat. Many people struggle with these veggies, but this way of cooking them persuades even their harshest critics.

RICH IN:
Glucosinolates
Inulin
Vitamin C

SERVES: 4
½ large broccoli, broken
  into small florets
500g (1lb 2oz) Brussels
  sprouts, halved
Olive oil, for roasting
1 large red onion, sliced
1 heaped teaspoon smoked
  sweet paprika
½ teaspoon garlic salt
1 teaspoon dried mixed herbs

ROASTED BRUSSELS SPROUTS, BROCCOLI AND RED ONION

Preheat the oven to 200°C (400°F), Gas Mark 6.

Place the broccoli and Brussels sprouts in a roasting tin, drizzle with a little olive oil and toss well. Place in the oven and roast for around 15 minutes.

Remove and add the sliced onion, paprika, garlic salt and dried herbs, then toss together well. Return to the oven for a further 20–25 minutes until all vegetables are soft and golden and crisp at the edges.

Serve immediately.

SERVES: 4
1 large red cabbage,
   thinly sliced
1 teaspoon fennel seeds
1 teaspoon allspice
5 star anise
3 cinnamon sticks
6–7 black peppercorns
500ml (18fl oz) red
   wine vinegar

*As simple as it gets, although you do have to be patient!
This is a great addition to sandwiches and wraps.*

SPICY PICKLED RED CABBAGE

Place all the ingredients in a large, sterilized, airtight jar. Mix together well and seal. Leave for 2–3 weeks before using.

Store in the fridge and use within 6–8 weeks for maximum crunchiness.

SERVES: 4
180g (6oz) brown rice
1 small carrot, cut into
   small dice
4 tablespoons fresh
   or frozen peas
1 tablespoon sweetcorn
Olive oil, for sautéing
1 spring onion, thinly sliced
2 teaspoons pomegranate
   seeds

This is a great side dish that will go with many of the recipes in this book. Brown rice on its own is a very nutritious grain, but the jewels give it an extra boost.

JEWELLED BROWN RICE

Cook the rice in a large pan of boiling water according to the packet instructions. Drain and set aside.

In a small saucepan over a medium heat, sauté the diced carrot, peas and sweetcorn in a little olive oil for 5 minutes until softened.

Add the cooked rice and take off the heat. Add the spring onion and pomegranate seeds and mix everything together well before serving.

RICH IN:
Carotenoids
Magnesium

SERVES: 4
3 large courgettes,
    thinly sliced at an angle
½ teaspoon smoked paprika
½ teaspoon za'atar
½ teaspoon ground turmeric
Pinch of garlic salt
Olive oil, for griddling
Black pepper

To garnish (optional)
Handful of micro salad
Herb leaves, such as mint,
    parsley and coriander

*This is a beautiful side for Mediterranean dishes
and is perfect for al fresco dining.*

SPICED GRIDDLED COURGETTES

Place the courgette slices in a bowl and sprinkle over
the spices and garlic salt.

Heat a griddle pan or frying pan over a high heat and
add a drizzle of olive oil. Griddle the courgette slices
for 4–6 minutes, turning frequently.

Garnish the courgettes with micro salad and a few herb
leaves, if using, add some black pepper, then serve.

This is a stunning side dish that is great with a roast dinner, or even served cold as the base of a salad.

SERVES: 4
2 beetroots, cut into wedges
2 parsnips, cut into quarters
  lengthways
2 large carrots, cut into
  quarters lengthways
Olive oil, for roasting
4 tablespoons balsamic
  vinegar
Large rosemary sprig,
  leaves picked
Salt

BALSAMIC ROASTED ROOTS

Preheat the oven to 200°C (400°F), Gas Mark 6.

Place the chopped vegetables in a roasting tin. Drizzle with olive oil and 1 tablespoon of the balsamic vinegar, and sprinkle over a pinch of salt.

Place in the oven to roast for 10 minutes. Remove, scatter over the rosemary and drizzle over another tablespoon of the balsamic vinegar. Toss well and return to the oven for another 15 minutes.

Remove, add a third tablespoon of the balsamic vinegar, toss well and return to the oven for another 10 minutes.

At this point, all the vegetables should be cooked and the balsamic caramelized. Add the final tablespoon of balsamic vinegar, toss well and leave to rest for a few minutes before serving.

B vitamins
Flavonoids
Iron
Magnesium
Zinc

SERVES: 4
180g (6oz) quinoa
2 tablespoons capers
Small bunch of flat-leaf
 parsley, roughly chopped
½ red onion, finely sliced

This is a great side for roasted veggies and traybakes.

QUINOA SALAD

Place the quinoa in a saucepan over a medium heat.
Cover with boiling water, reduce the heat and simmer
for 20 minutes until cooked. Drain.

Add the capers, parsley and red onion, and mix well
before serving.

SERVES: 4
3 large parsnips, cut into
quarters lengthways
Olive oil, for drizzling
1 tablespoon maple syrup
2 teaspoons wholegrain
mustard
Salt

This is one of my favourite sides; it goes especially well with Christmas dinner!

MAPLE-MUSTARD PARSNIPS

Preheat the oven to 200°C (400°F), Gas Mark 6.

Place the parsnips in a roasting tin. Drizzle with olive oil, add a pinch of salt, toss well and roast for 25 minutes.

Meanwhile, mix the maple syrup and wholegrain mustard together.

Remove the parsnips from the oven, drizzle over the maple-mustard mixture and toss to ensure the parsnips are covered. Return to the oven for a further 15–20 minutes until the parsnips are golden and crisp at the edges, and the dressing has caramelized.

Serve immediately.

SERVES: 4
½ celeriac, diced
4 large carrots, diced
1 small swede, diced
Olive oil, for roasting
½ teaspoon vegetable
   stock powder
½ teaspoon garlic salt
½ tablespoon vegan butter

This is a lovely flavoursome alternative to mashed potatoes, and perfect as a winter side.

THREE-ROOT MASH

Preheat the oven to 200°C (400°F), Gas Mark 6.

Place the diced celeriac, carrots and swede in a roasting tin and drizzle with a little olive oil. Sprinkle over the stock powder and garlic salt, then toss.

Roast for 35–40 minutes until softened and golden at the edges.

Remove from the roasting tin and transfer to a bowl or saucepan. Add the vegan butter and mash.

Serve immediately.

SERVES: 4
2 garlic cloves,
   finely chopped
1 small red chilli,
   deseeded and chopped
Olive oil, for sautéing
500g (1lb 2oz) Brussels
   sprouts, shredded or
   very thinly sliced
1 tablespoon maple syrup
Salt

Who said Brussels sprouts need to be boiled to death and eaten only at Christmas? These super-healthy vegetables are really versatile, and this is a great way to prepare them.

CHILLI-MAPLE SHREDDED SPROUTS

In a frying pan over a medium heat, sauté the garlic and chilli in a little olive oil, along with a good pinch of salt, for 2–3 minutes.

Add the shredded Brussels sprouts and sauté for 8–10 minutes until softened.

Add the maple syrup and sauté for another 2 minutes before serving.

RICH IN:
Flavonoids
Glucosinolates
Vitamin C

This nutrient-dense coleslaw is great on a baked potato or in a sandwich.

SERVES: 4
½ small red cabbage
1 red apple, cored
1 red onion
3 tablespoons natural
   coconut yogurt
1 teaspoon wholegrain
   mustard
Salt and black pepper

RED SLAW

Thinly slice the cabbage, apple and onion, then place in a bowl.

Add the coconut yogurt and mustard, season with salt and black pepper and mix everything together well.

Serve immediately.

RICH IN:
Glucosinolates
Magnesium
Vitamin C

SERVES: 4
1 large cauliflower, broken
  into small florets, inner
  leaves left attached
Olive oil, for roasting
½ teaspoon mild curry powder
½ teaspoon garam masala
¼ teaspoon garlic salt
Handful of coriander leaves,
  to garnish (optional)

*I have to admit, until recently I hated cauliflower.
Plain cooked cauliflower just doesn't do it for me,
but the day I tried it roasted...game changer!*

ROASTED SPICED CAULIFLOWER

Preheat the oven to 200°C (400°F), Gas Mark 6.

Add the cauliflower to a saucepan of boiling water
over a medium heat. Simmer for 2–3 minutes to
lightly but not completely cook, then drain and
allow to steam dry.

Place the cauliflower in a roasting tin. Drizzle
over some olive oil and toss well. Sprinkle over
the spices and garlic salt, and toss again.

Roast for around 20 minutes until golden and
crisp at the edges. Garnish with the coriander
leaves, if using, and serve.

RECIPES BY NUTRIENT

Below is a handy list of the recipes in this book arranged by nutrient – a great tool for ensuring that your diet is as nutritionally balanced and diverse as possible.

Anthocyanins
Black bean, corn, jalapeño, avocado
  and red onion salad (see page 81)
Black bean, courgette and kale chilli
  (see page 116)

Beta-carotene
Kale salad with almond chilli sauce
  (see page 76)
Mango, chilli and coriander lettuce wraps
  (see page 78)
Courgette and carrot noodles with green
  herb dressing (see page 82)
Cauliflower 'rice' bibimbap (see page 85)
Kelp noodle salad with miso sesame
  dressing (see page 86)
Sweet potato, red lentil, coconut and ginger
  soup (see page 98)
Red lentil and roasted carrot dip
  (see page 105)
Cannellini bean and roasted pepper dip
  (see page 109)
Black bean, courgette and kale chilli
  (see page 116)
Sweet potato and coconut dhal (see page 119)
Creamy tomato and chilli gnocchi
  (see page 125)
Moroccan-style vegetable stew
  (see page 130)
Green masala with peas, carrots and
  courgettes (see page 134)
Pepper and tofu stir-fry (see page 151)
Griddled peach, rocket, spinach and
  pomegranate salad (see page 158)
Spiced squash traybake with couscous
  (see page 164)

Pasta with tomato and chilli sauce
  (see page 167)
Twice-baked sweet potato boats (see page 170)
Orzo with roasted vegetable sauce
  (see page 172)
Roasted baby carrots on turmeric butter
  bean purée (see page 180)
Red onion, sweet potato and spinach
  barlotto (see page 183)
Balsamic pepper and red onion traybake
  with lentil salad and carrot-ginger purée
  (see page 188)
Ratatouille-topped baked potato
  (see page 192)
Lentil and chickpea shepherd's pie
  (see page 199)
Miso aubergine on chilli-ginger carrot mash
  with garlic pak choi (see page 202)
Jewelled brown rice (see page 213)
Three-root mash (see page 222)

Betacyanin
Beetroot, walnut and wasabi dip
  (see page 100)
Beetroot, celeriac and chickpea roast
  (see page 169)
Roasted beetroot on white onion and
  horseradish purée (see page 184)
Balsamic roasted roots (see page 217)

B vitamins
Chickpea chopped salad (see page 80)
Sweet potato, red lentil, coconut and
  ginger soup (see page 98)
Red lentil and roasted carrot dip
  (see page 105)

Roasted mushroom tacos (see page 144)
Sweet potato, red onion and cherry tomato
    traybake (see page 174)
Spiced griddled courgettes (see page 214)
Balsamic roasted roots (see page 217)

Fibre
Fennel and orange salad (see page 74)
Chickpea chopped salad (see page 80)
Curried black bean soup (see page 92)
Sweet potato, red lentil, coconut and
    ginger soup (see page 98)
Red lentil and roasted carrot dip
    (see page 105)
Caponata with couscous (see page 133)
Jewelled brown rice (see page 213)
Three-root mash (see page 222)

Flavonoids
Fennel and orange salad (see page 74)
Mango, chilli and coriander lettuce wraps
    (see page 78)
Roasted tomato and red pepper soup
    (see page 90)
Curried black bean soup (see page 92)
Gorgeous gazpacho (see page 96)
Spicy sesame maple soba noodles
    (see page 121)·
Caponata with couscous (see page 133)
Mexican wrap (see page 140)
Peanut and coconut aubergine (see page 143)
Tofu, broccoli and red onion fried rice
    (see page 146)
Spiced aubergine mash-up on toast
    (see page 148)
Pepper and tofu stir-fry (see page 151)
Linguine with sautéed leeks and fennel
    (see page 152)
Fig, radicchio and roasted red onion salad
    with balsamic dressing (see page 155)
Spiced squash traybake with couscous
    (see page 164)
Sweet potato, red onion and cherry tomato
    traybake (see page 174)

Lentil-stuffed aubergine rolls with tahini
    sauce (see page 178)
Red onion, sweet potato and spinach
    barlotto (see page 183)
Roasted fennel, 'creamed' corn, crispy cavolo
    nero and pickled red onions (see page 187)
Balsamic pepper and red onion traybake
    with lentil salad and carrot-ginger purée
    (see page 188)
Ratatouille-topped baked potato
    (see page 192)
Baked aubergine and wilted kale with
    tahini sauce (see page 193)
Classic green curry (see page 195)
Aubergine and lentil lasagne (see page 196)
Miso aubergine on chilli-ginger carrot mash
    with garlic pak choi (see page 202)
Spicy pickled red cabbage (see page 212)
Quinoa salad (see page 218)
Red slaw (see page 225)

Glucosinolates
Kale salad with almond chilli sauce
    (see page 76)
Cauliflower 'rice' bibimbap (see page 85)
Tofu, broccoli and red onion fried rice
    (see page 146)
Griddled peach, rocket, spinach and
    pomegranate salad (see page 158)
Easy cauliflower and pea curry
    (see page 166)
Curried new potato and broccoli roast
    (see page 175)
Moroccan-spiced cauliflower steaks
    (see page 200)
Roasted broccoli with tahini drizzle
    (see page 206)
Roasted Brussels sprouts, broccoli and
    red onion (see page 211)
Spicy pickled red cabbage (see page 212)
Chilli-maple shredded sprouts
    (see page 223)
Red slaw (see page 225)
Roasted spiced cauliflower (see page 226)

Immunomodulatory polysaccharides

Inulin

Iron

Isoflavones

Lignans

Lutein

Lycopene

Magnesium

Oleic acid

Oligosaccharides

Sweet potato, red lentil, coconut and ginger
  soup (see page 98)
Cannellini bean and roasted pepper dip
  (see page 109)
Black bean, courgette and kale chilli
  (see page 116)
Mexican wrap (see page 140)
Black-eyed bean, tomato, red onion
  and spinach sauté (see page 147)
Roasted baby carrots on turmeric butter
  bean purée (see page 180)
Balsamic roasted roots (see page 217)
Maple-mustard parsnips (see page 221)
Three-root mash (see page 222)

Potassium
Kale salad with almond chilli sauce
  (see page 76)
Olive and artichoke spread (see page 99)
Beetroot, walnut and wasabi dip
  (see page 100)
Roasted fennel, 'creamed' corn, crispy cavolo
  nero and pickled red onions (see page 187)

Selenium
Spicy sesame maple soba noodles
  (see page 121)
Tofu shiitake rice noodles (see page 137)
Tofu, broccoli and red onion fried rice
  (see page 146)
Pepper and tofu stir-fry (see page 151)
Fig, radicchio and roasted red onion salad
  with balsamic dressing (see page 155)
Baked tofu satay (see page 162)
Twice-baked sweet potato boats
  (see page 170)
Lentil-stuffed aubergine rolls with
  tahini sauce (see page 178)
Stuffed field mushrooms on white bean
  cassoulet (see page 190)
Baked aubergine and wilted kale with
  tahini sauce (see page 193)
Roasted broccoli with tahini drizzle
  (see page 206)

Soluble fibre
Sweet potato, red lentil, coconut and ginger
  soup (see page 98)
A lean classic hummus (see page 108)
Sweet potato and coconut dhal (see page 119)
Spinach dhal (see page 120)
Spaghetti with Puy lentil Bolognese
  (see page 129)
Moroccan-style vegetable stew (see page 130)
Beetroot, celeriac and chickpea roast
  (see page 169)
Twice-baked sweet potato boats
  (see page 170)
Curried new potato and broccoli roast
  (see page 175)
Balsamic pepper and red onion traybake
  with lentil salad and carrot-ginger purée
  (see page 188)
Stuffed field mushrooms on white bean
  cassoulet (see page 190)
Aubergine and lentil lasagne (see page 196)
Lentil and chickpea shepherd's pie
  (see page 199)

Vitamin C
Fennel and orange salad (see page 74)
Mango, chilli and coriander lettuce
  wraps (see page 78)
Roasted tomato and red pepper soup
  (see page 90)
Carrot, orange and caraway soup
  (see page 95)
Gorgeous gazpacho (see page 96)
Avocado, sun-dried tomato and basil dip
  (see page 102)
A lean classic hummus (see page 108)
Cannellini bean and roasted pepper dip
  (see page 109)
Nutty sweet potato and spinach curry
  (see page 112)
Sun-dried tomato and red pepper risotto
  (see page 126)
Roasted mushroom tacos (see page 144)
Pepper and tofu stir-fry (see page 151)

Fig, radicchio and roasted red onion salad
with balsamic dressing (see page 155)
Curried beans and greens (see page 156)
Griddled peach, rocket, spinach and
pomegranate salad (see page 158)
Orzo with roasted vegetable sauce
(see page 172)
Roasted beetroot on white onion and
horseradish purée (see page 184)
Roasted fennel, 'creamed' corn, crispy cavolo
nero and pickled red onions (see page 187)
Ratatouille-topped baked potato (see page 190)
Moroccan-spiced cauliflower steaks
(see page 200)
Roasted broccoli with tahini drizzle
(see page 206)
Avocado 'mayo' (see page 208)
Roasted Brussels sprouts, broccoli and
red onion (see page 211)
Jewelled brown rice (see page 213)
Maple-mustard parsnips (see page 221)
Chilli-maple shredded sprouts (see page 223)
Red slaw (see page 225)
Roasted spiced cauliflower (see page 226)

Vitamin E
Black bean, corn, jalapeño, avocado and
red onion salad (see page 81)
Courgette and carrot noodles with green
herb dressing (see page 82)
Olive and artichoke spread (see page 99)
Avocado, sun-dried tomato and basil dip
(see page 102)
Nutty sweet potato and spinach curry
(see page 112)
Penne with courgettes, spinach and walnut
pesto (see page 115)
Mexican wrap (see page 140)
Peanut and coconut aubergine (see page 143)
Roasted mushroom tacos (see page 144)
Baked tofu satay (see page 162)
Lentil-stuffed aubergine rolls with tahini
sauce (see page 178)
Avocado 'mayo' (see page 208)

Vitamin K
Kale salad with almond chilli sauce
(see page 76)
Avocado, sun-dried tomato and basil dip
(see page 102)
Roasted mushroom and miso sandwich
filler (see page 106)
Black bean, courgette and kale chilli
(see page 116)
Green masala with peas, carrots and
courgettes (see page 134)
Roasted fennel, 'creamed' corn, crispy cavolo
nero and pickled red onions (see page 187)
Baked aubergine and wilted kale with tahini
sauce (see page 193)
Avocado 'mayo' (see page 208)
Chilli-maple shredded sprouts (see page 223)

Zinc
Chickpea chopped salad (see page 80)
Penne with courgettes, spinach and walnut
pesto (see page 115)
Creamy tomato and chilli gnocchi
(see page 125)
Spaghetti with Puy lentil Bolognese
(see page 129)
Moroccan-style vegetable stew
(see page 130)
Mexican wrap (see page 140)
Twice-baked sweet potato boats
(see page 170)
Lentil-stuffed aubergine rolls with tahini
sauce (see page 178)
Roasted baby carrots on turmeric butter
bean purée (see page 180)
Stuffed field mushrooms on white bean
cassoulet (see page 190)
Baked aubergine and wilted kale with tahini
sauce (see page 193)
Classic green curry (see page 195)
Aubergine and lentil lasagne (see page 196)
Lentil and chickpea shepherd's pie
(see page 199)
Quinoa salad (see page 218)

REFERENCES

1. van de Wouw M, Schellekens H, Dinan T G, Cryan J F. (2017). 'Microbiota–Gut–Brain Axis: Modulator of Host Metabolism and Appetite', *The Journal of Nutrition*, 147 (5), pages 727–45. https://doi.org/10.3945/jn.116.240481

2. Chambers E S, Viardot A, Psichas A, et al. (2015). 'Effects of targeted delivery of propionate to the human colon on appetite regulation, body weight maintenance and adiposity in overweight adults', *Gut*, 64, pages 1744–54. https://doi.org/10.1136/gutjnl-2014-307913

3. Kumar Singh A, Cabral C, Kumar R, et al. (2019). 'Beneficial Effects of Dietary Polyphenols on Gut Microbiota and Strategies to Improve Delivery Efficiency', *Nutrients*, 11 (9), page 2216. https://doi.org/10.3390/nu11092216

4. Lamport D J, Pal D, Moutsiana C, Field D T, Williams C M, Spencer J P, Butler L T. (2015). 'The effect of flavanol-rich cocoa on cerebral perfusion in healthy older adults during conscious resting state: a placebo controlled, crossover, acute trial', *Psychopharmacology* (Berl), 232 (17), pages 3227–34. https://doi.org/10.1007/s00213-015-3972-4

5. Rogerson D, Maçãs D, Milner M, Liu Y, Klonizakis M. (2018). 'Contrasting Effects of Short-Term Mediterranean and Vegan Diets on Microvascular Function and Cholesterol in Younger Adults: A Comparative Pilot Study', *Nutrients*, 10 (12), page 1897. https://doi.org/10.3390/nu10121897

6. Vetvicka V, Vannucci L, Sima P, Richter J. (2019). 'Beta Glucan: Supplement or Drug? From Laboratory to Clinical Trials', *Molecules*, 24 (7), page 1251. https://doi.org/10.3390/molecules24071251

UK–US GLOSSARY OF TERMS

Ingredients

aubergine – eggplant
beetroot – beets
broad beans – fava beans
butter beans – lima beans
cannellini beans – white kidney beans
celeriac – celery root
chickpeas – garbanzo beans
coriander (fresh) – cilantro
courgettes – zucchini
pak choi – bok choy
peppers (red/green/yellow) – bell peppers
plain flour – all-purpose flour

spring onions – scallions
stock – broth
swede – rutabaga
long-stem broccoli – broccolini
tomato purée – tomato paste

Equipment

baking tin – baking pan
griddle pan – grill pan
grill – broiler
tin foil – aluminum foil
roasting tin – roasting pan

INDEX